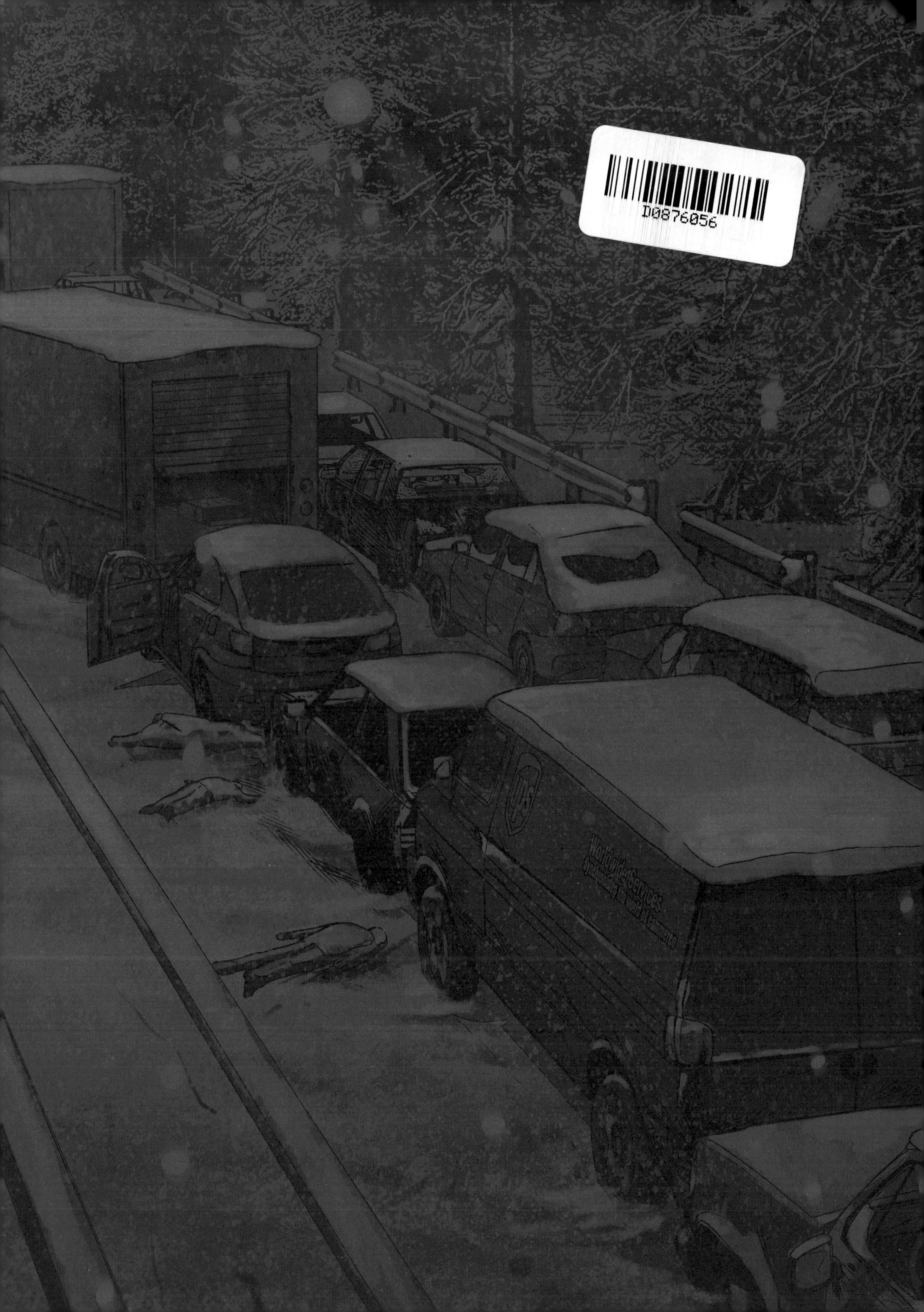
Worldwide Services

NIGHT OF THE LIVING DEAD

NIGHT OF THE LIVING DEAD

1: The Sins of the Father

STORY
JEAN-LUC ISTIN

ART
ELIA BONETTI

COLOR
DIGIKORE STUDIOS

FIREFLY BOOKS

A FIREFLY BOOK

Published by Firefly Books Ltd. 2016

Original French edition copyright © 2014 éditions Glénat / Vents d'Ouest
This translated edition copyright © 2016 Firefly Books

First printing

Publisher Cataloging-in-Publication Data (U.S.)

Names: Istin, Jean-Luc, author. | Bonetti, Elia, 1983-, illustrator. | Hahnenburger, Ivanka, translator.
Title: Night of the living dead. Volume 1, The sins of the father / Jean-Luc Istin ; illustrator, Elia Bonetti ; translator Ivanka Hahnenburger.
Description: Richmond Hill, Ontario, Canada : Firefly Books, 2016. | Previously published by Glenat Publishing, Grenoble, France, 2014 as "La Nuit des Morts Vivants," Volume 1. | Summary: "A modern rewrite of the classic cult movie, this vivid graphic novel brings the dead back to life through the eyes of Lizbeth. When visiting the grave of their adoptive parents with her brother, Lizbeth comes face to face with countless zombies. The siblings find shelter, but Lizbeth is fearful about what might have happened to her two children and husband" — Provided by publisher.
Identifiers: ISBN 978-1-77085-799-5 (hardcover)
Subjects: LCSH: Zombies – Comic books, strips, etc. | Graphic novels.
Classification: LCC PN6727.I885N544 | DDC 741.5973 – dc23

Library and Archives Canada Cataloguing in Publication

Istin, Jean-Luc
[Fautes du père. English]
        The sins of the father / story, Jean-Luc Istin ; art, Elia Bonetti ; color, Digikore Studios.
(Night of the living dead ; 1)
Translation of: Les fautes du père.
Graphic novelization of (work): Night of the living dead (Motion picture : 1968)
ISBN 978-1-77085-799-5 (hardback)
        1. Zombies—Comic books, strips, etc. 2. Graphic novels.
I. Bonetti, Elia, 1983-, illustrator II. Title. III. Title: Fautes du père. English . IV. Title: Night of the living dead (Motion picture : 1968). V. Series: Night of the living dead (Series) ; 1

PN6747.I77F3913 2016   741.5'944   C2016-901036-8

Published in the United States by
Firefly Books (U.S.) Inc.
P.O. Box 1338, Ellicott Station
Buffalo, New York 14205

Published in Canada by
Firefly Books Ltd.
50 Staples Avenue, Unit 1
Richmond Hill, Ontario L4B 0A7

Cover illustration: Ronan Toulhoat
Translation: Ivanka Hahnenberger

Printed in China

Thanks to Elia, who helped make this old dream a reality.
Thanks to Manik for his fabulous work!
Thanks to Valérie, who, luckily for us, likes the living dead!
And especially thank you to the fabulous George Romero, the inventor of the modern zombie, which terrorized my adolescence, to my great pleasure!
Working on this book gave me indefinable joy. Thanks again, George!

J.-L. ISTIN

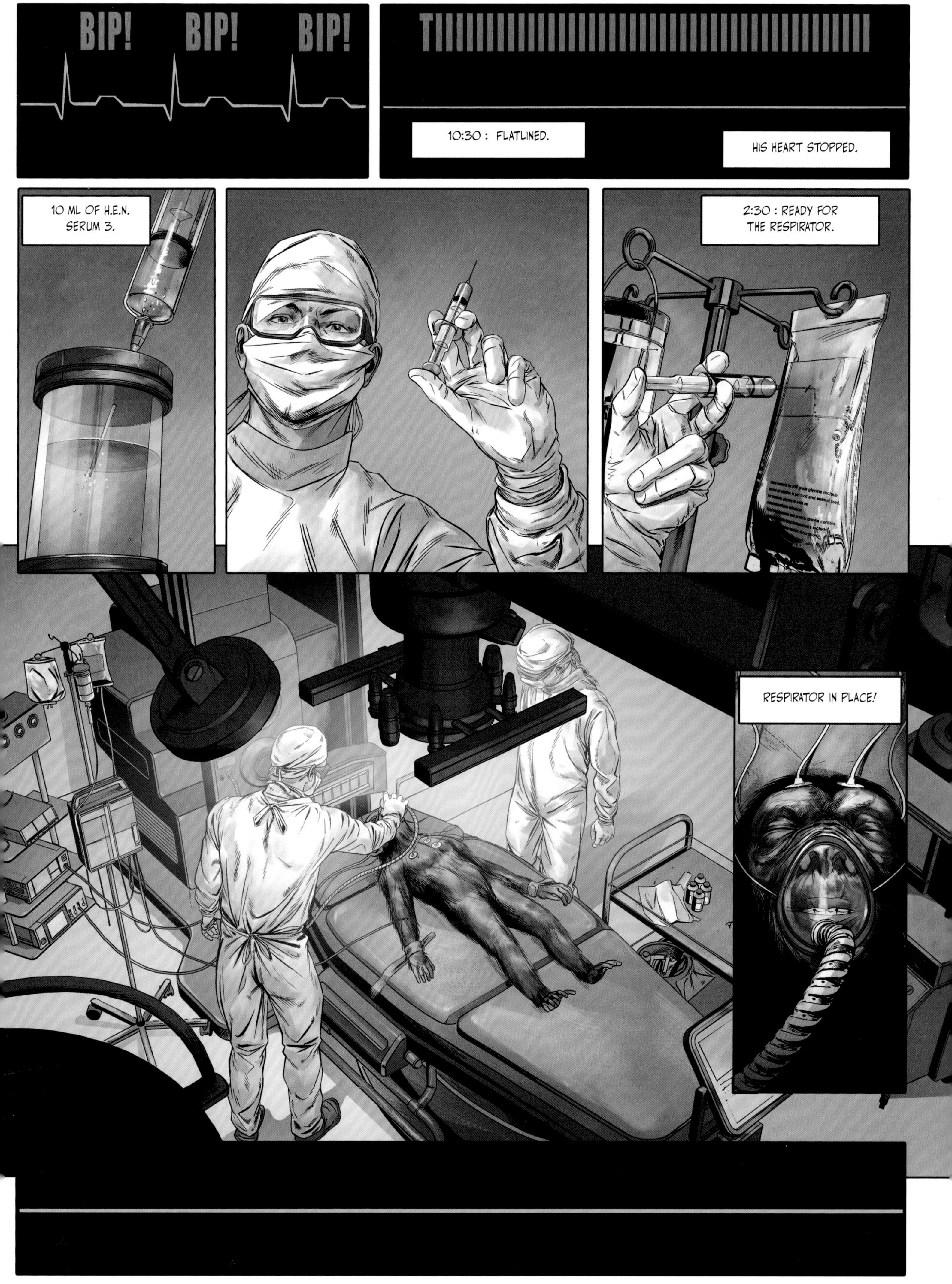
BIP! BIP! BIP!
TIIIIIIIIIIIIIIIIIIIIIIIIIIIIIIIIIIIIIIIIIIIIIIIII
10:30 : FLATLINED.
HIS HEART STOPPED.
10 ML OF H.E.N. SERUM 3.
2:30 : READY FOR THE RESPIRATOR.
RESPIRATOR IN PLACE!

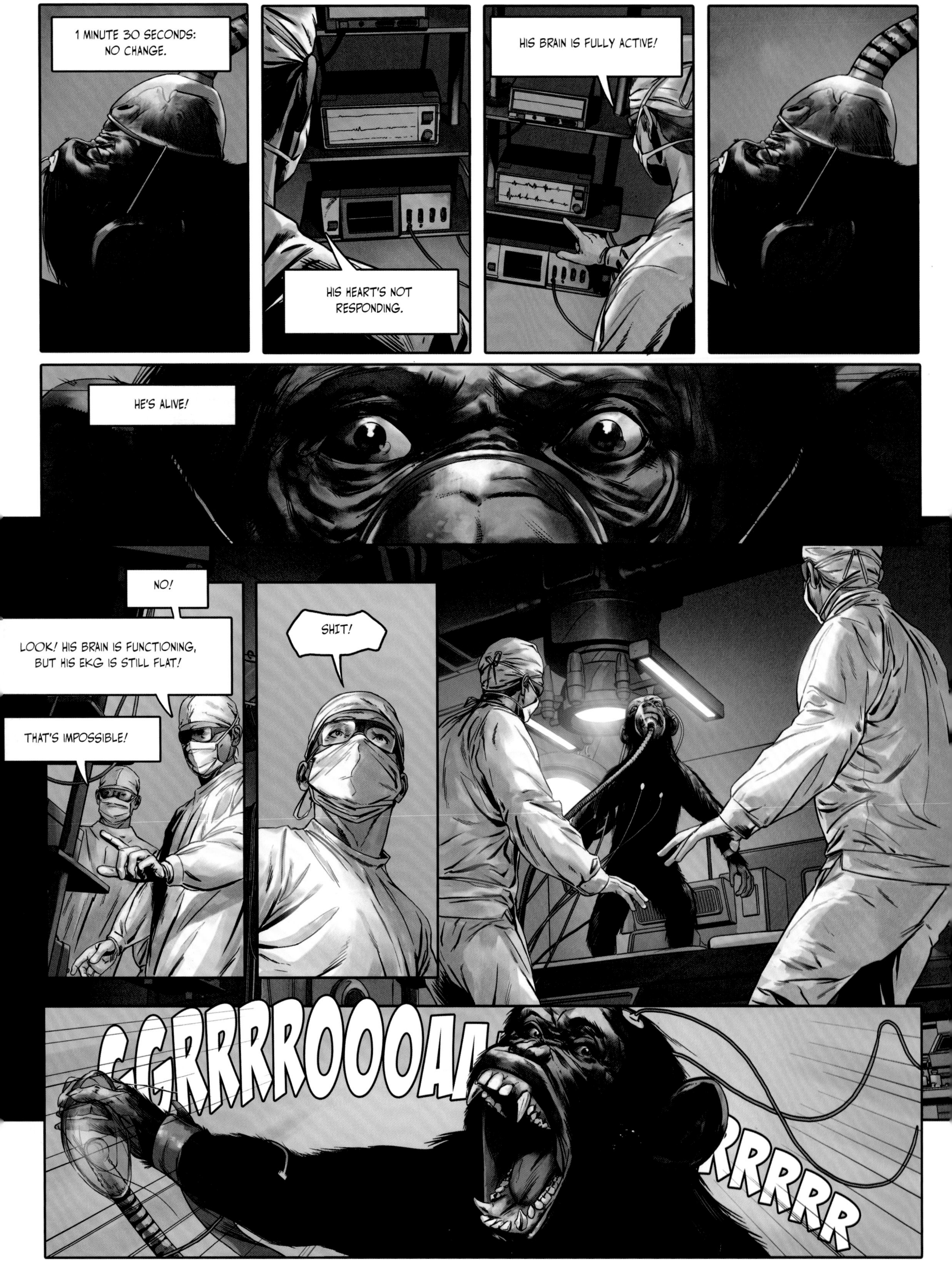
1 MINUTE 30 SECONDS: NO CHANGE.
HIS HEART'S NOT RESPONDING.
HIS BRAIN IS FULLY ACTIVE!
HE'S ALIVE!
NO!
LOOK! HIS BRAIN IS FUNCTIONING, BUT HIS EKG IS STILL FLAT!
THAT'S IMPOSSIBLE!
SHIT!
GRRRROOOA
RRRRR

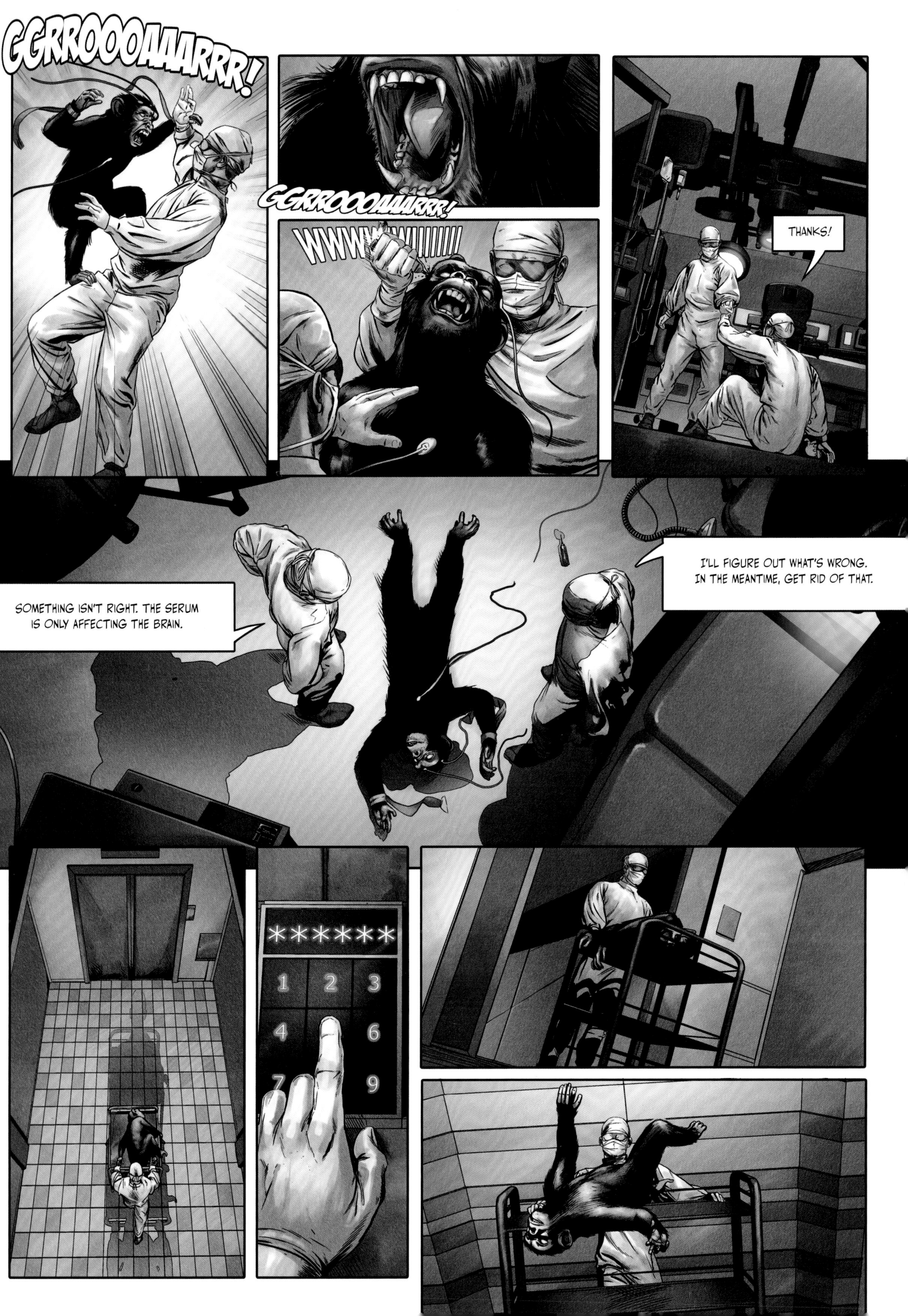
GGRROOOAAARRR!
GGRROOOAAARRR!
WWWWWIIIIIII
THANKS!
SOMETHING ISN'T RIGHT. THE SERUM IS ONLY AFFECTING THE BRAIN.
I'LL FIGURE OUT WHAT'S WRONG. IN THE MEANTIME, GET RID OF THAT.
******
1 2 3
4 6
7 9

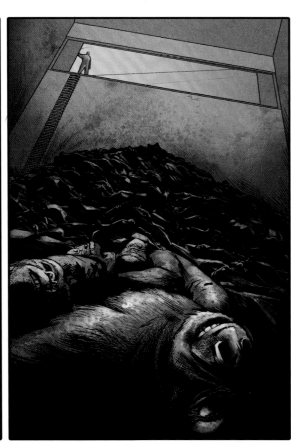

ARE YOU AFRAID OF DEATH?

ILLENES KORP.

OBVIOUSLY I'M AFRAID.

WHO ISN'T AFRAID OF DYING?

DYING DOESN'T SCARE ME.

I DON'T BELIEVE YOU.

WHAT IS IT EXACTLY THAT SCARES YOU ABOUT DYING?

THE SKIN DECOMPOSING, DECAY, EMPTINESS, NOTHINGNESS.

AND THE IDEA OF A SOUL THAT SURVIVES THE BODY?

I WOULD REALLY LIKE TO BELIEVE THAT, BUT NO. I ALWAYS COME BACK TO WHAT I FEEL. AND I AM HAUNTED BY THE THOUGHT OF PEOPLE CLOSE TO ME DYING. EVERY DAY I AM AFRAID THAT SOMETHING IS GOING TO HAPPEN TO THEM.

LIZBETH, I WOULD LIKE TO SUGGEST A HYPNOSIS SESSION.

WHY?

BECAUSE THERE'S NO DOUBT THAT THERE ARE BURIED MEMORIES BEHIND YOUR OBSESSION WITH DEATH. YOU DON'T REMEMBER YOUR REAL PARENTS. YOU SAY, YOUR LIFE BEGAN AT THE AGE OF SEVEN. BUT WHAT ABOUT BEFORE ...

I DON'T KNOW. I CAME HERE TO PLEASE MY HUSBAND. I DON'T BELIEVE ANY OF THIS WILL HELP ANYTHING. WORK IS HELPING ME HEAL ...

DON'T YOU WANT TO KNOW MORE ABOUT THE PART OF YOUR LIFE THAT YOU'VE BEEN RUNNING AWAY FROM FOR SUCH A LONG TIME? THE PART YOU HAVE HIDDEN MORE OR LESS CONSCIOUSLY? AREN'T YOU CURIOUS TO KNOW MORE?

OK ...

WHEN DO WE START?

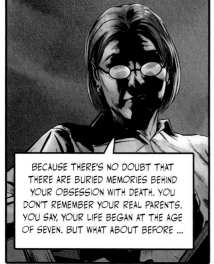

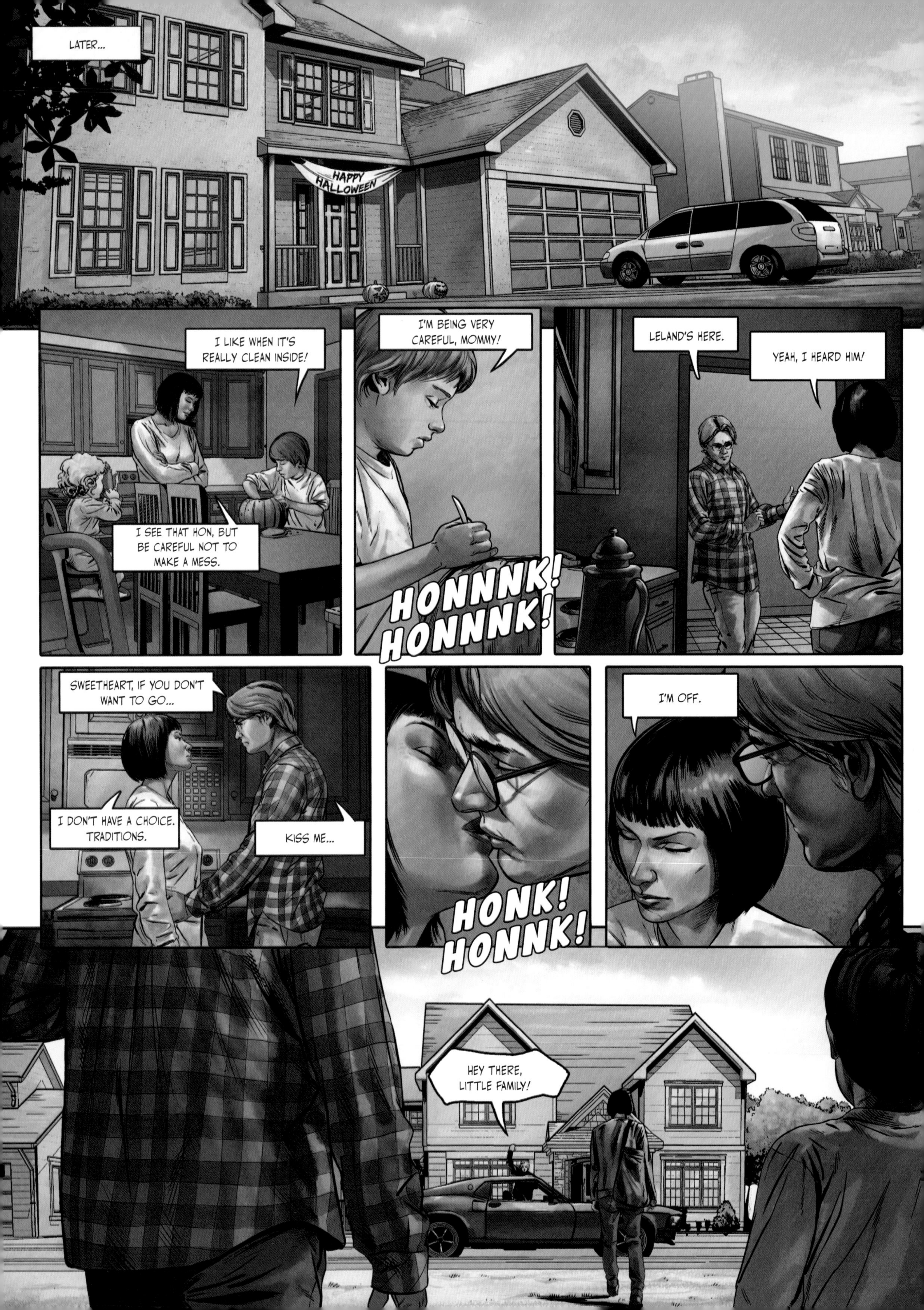
LATER...
I LIKE WHEN IT'S REALLY CLEAN INSIDE!
I SEE THAT HON, BUT BE CAREFUL NOT TO MAKE A MESS.
I'M BEING VERY CAREFUL, MOMMY!
HONNNK! HONNNK!
LELAND'S HERE.
YEAH, I HEARD HIM!
SWEETHEART, IF YOU DON'T WANT TO GO...
I DON'T HAVE A CHOICE. TRADITIONS.
KISS ME...
HONK! HONNK!
I'M OFF.
HEY THERE, LITTLE FAMILY!

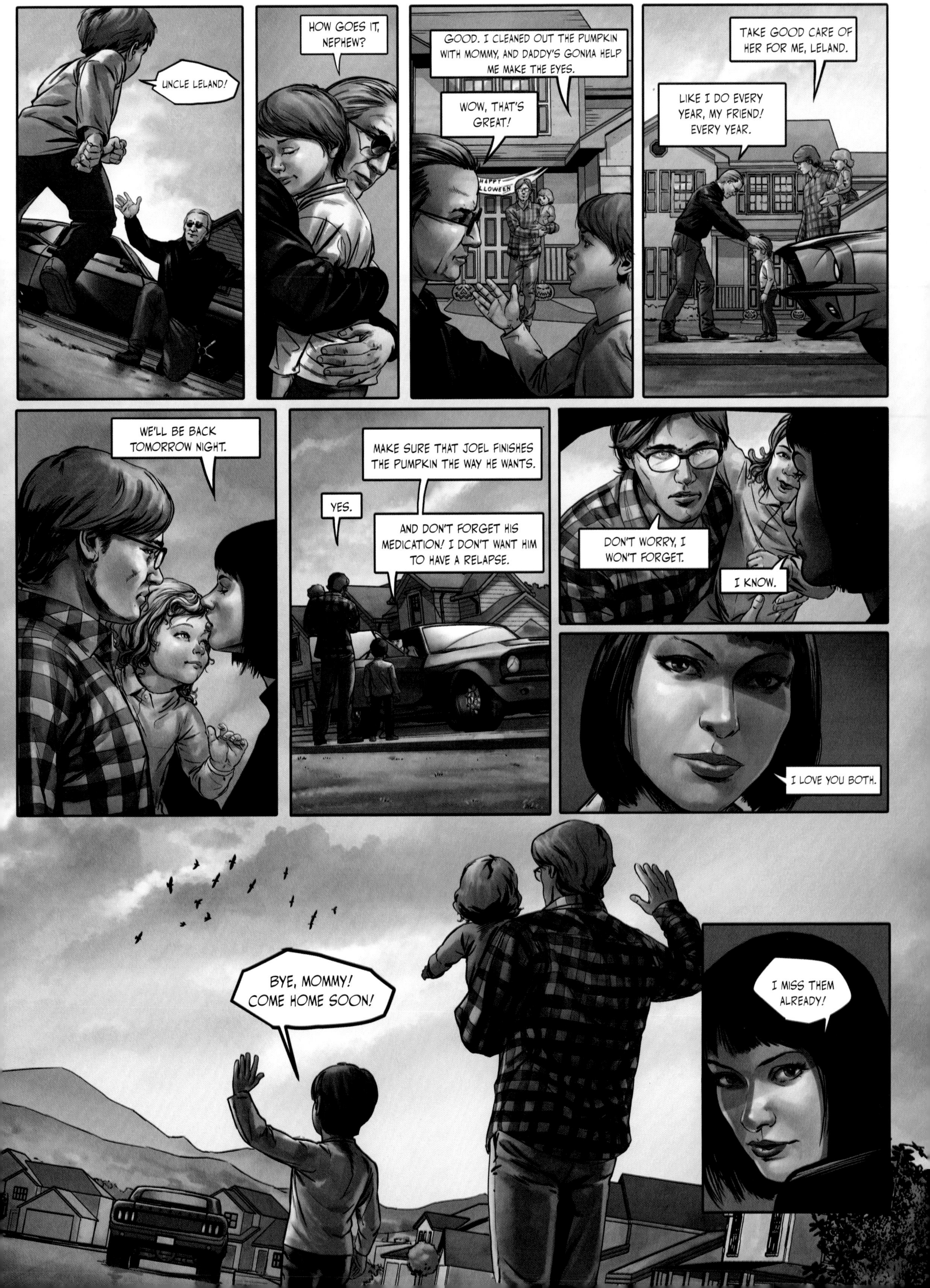
UNCLE LELAND!
HOW GOES IT, NEPHEW?
GOOD. I CLEANED OUT THE PUMPKIN WITH MOMMY, AND DADDY'S GONNA HELP ME MAKE THE EYES.
WOW, THAT'S GREAT!
HAPPY HALLOWEEN
TAKE GOOD CARE OF HER FOR ME, LELAND.
LIKE I DO EVERY YEAR, MY FRIEND! EVERY YEAR.
WE'LL BE BACK TOMORROW NIGHT.
MAKE SURE THAT JOEL FINISHES THE PUMPKIN THE WAY HE WANTS.
YES.
AND DON'T FORGET HIS MEDICATION! I DON'T WANT HIM TO HAVE A RELAPSE.
DON'T WORRY, I WON'T FORGET.
I KNOW.
I LOVE YOU BOTH.
BYE, MOMMY! COME HOME SOON!
I MISS THEM ALREADY!

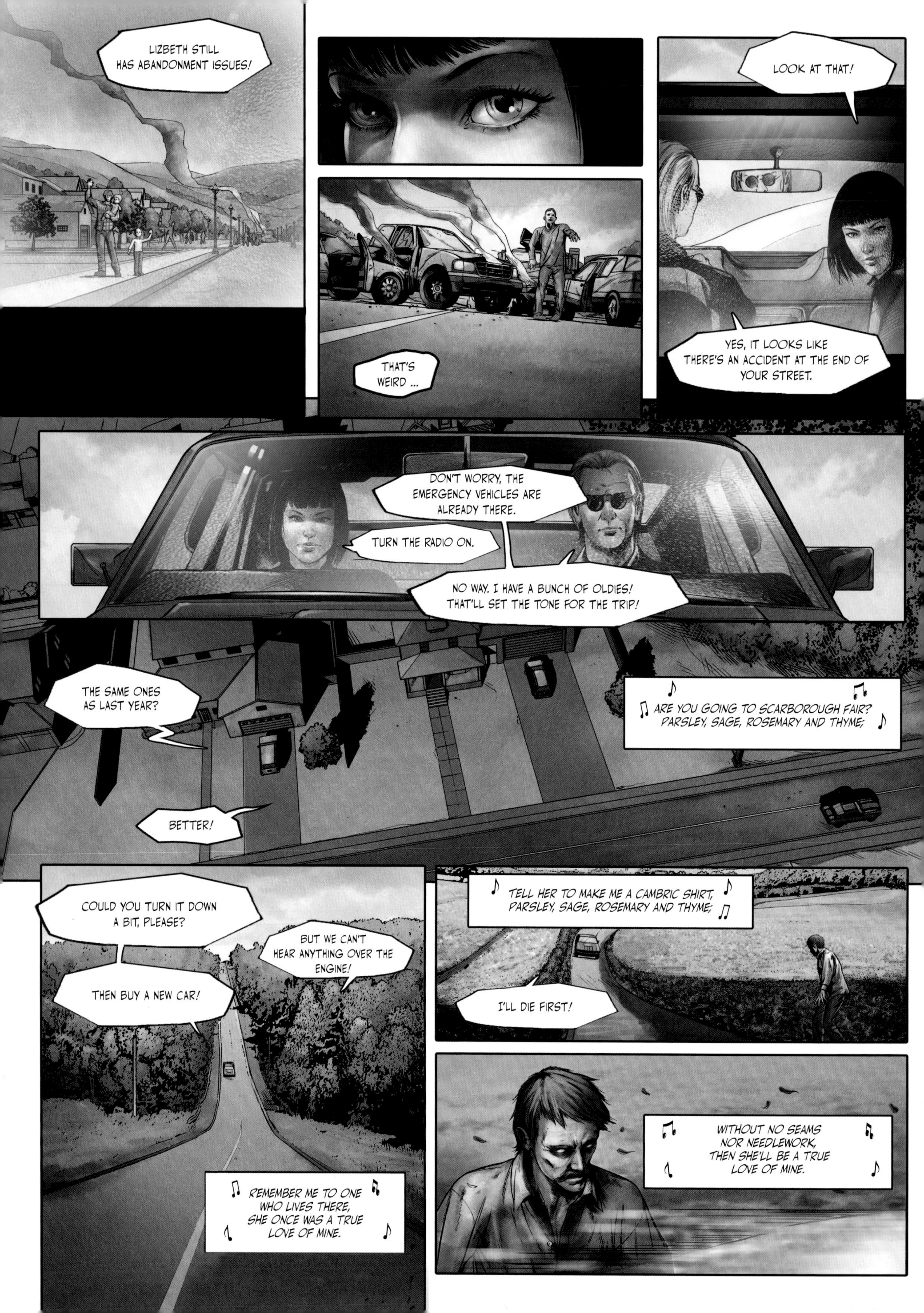

LIZBETH STILL HAS ABANDONMENT ISSUES!
LOOK AT THAT!
THAT'S WEIRD ...
YES, IT LOOKS LIKE THERE'S AN ACCIDENT AT THE END OF YOUR STREET.
DON'T WORRY, THE EMERGENCY VEHICLES ARE ALREADY THERE.
TURN THE RADIO ON.
NO WAY. I HAVE A BUNCH OF OLDIES! THAT'LL SET THE TONE FOR THE TRIP!
THE SAME ONES AS LAST YEAR?
BETTER!
ARE YOU GOING TO SCARBOROUGH FAIR? PARSLEY, SAGE, ROSEMARY AND THYME;
COULD YOU TURN IT DOWN A BIT, PLEASE?
BUT WE CAN'T HEAR ANYTHING OVER THE ENGINE!
THEN BUY A NEW CAR!
REMEMBER ME TO ONE WHO LIVES THERE, SHE ONCE WAS A TRUE LOVE OF MINE.
TELL HER TO MAKE ME A CAMBRIC SHIRT, PARSLEY, SAGE, ROSEMARY AND THYME;
I'LL DIE FIRST!
WITHOUT NO SEAMS NOR NEEDLEWORK, THEN SHE'LL BE A TRUE LOVE OF MINE.

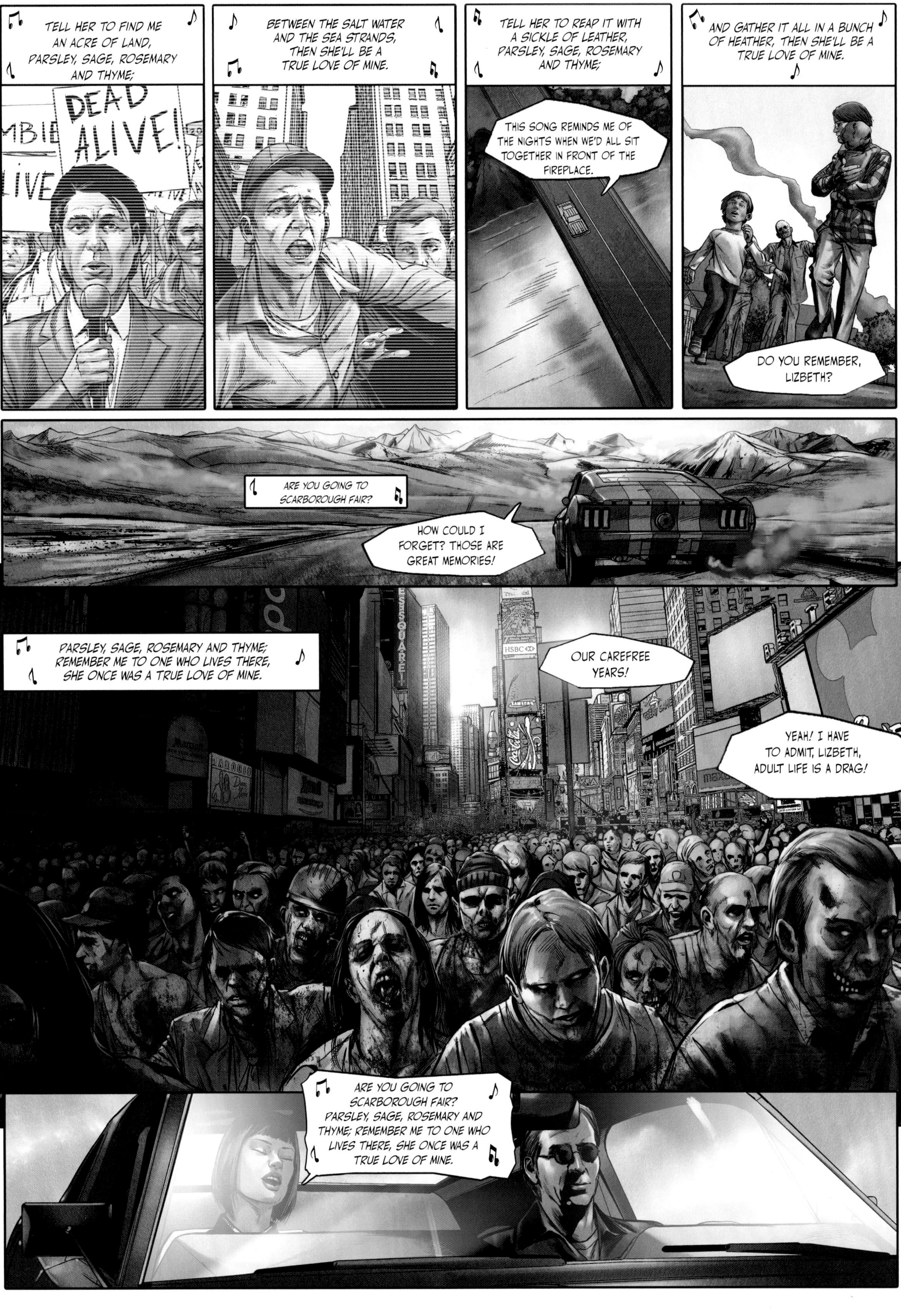
TELL HER TO FIND ME AN ACRE OF LAND, PARSLEY, SAGE, ROSEMARY AND THYME;
DEAD ALIVE!
BETWEEN THE SALT WATER AND THE SEA STRANDS, THEN SHE'LL BE A TRUE LOVE OF MINE.
TELL HER TO REAP IT WITH A SICKLE OF LEATHER, PARSLEY, SAGE, ROSEMARY AND THYME;
THIS SONG REMINDS ME OF THE NIGHTS WHEN WE'D ALL SIT TOGETHER IN FRONT OF THE FIREPLACE.
AND GATHER IT ALL IN A BUNCH OF HEATHER, THEN SHE'LL BE A TRUE LOVE OF MINE.
DO YOU REMEMBER, LIZBETH?
ARE YOU GOING TO SCARBOROUGH FAIR?
HOW COULD I FORGET? THOSE ARE GREAT MEMORIES!
PARSLEY, SAGE, ROSEMARY AND THYME; REMEMBER ME TO ONE WHO LIVES THERE, SHE ONCE WAS A TRUE LOVE OF MINE.
OUR CAREFREE YEARS!
YEAH! I HAVE TO ADMIT, LIZBETH, ADULT LIFE IS A DRAG!
ARE YOU GOING TO SCARBOROUGH FAIR? PARSLEY, SAGE, ROSEMARY AND THYME; REMEMBER ME TO ONE WHO LIVES THERE, SHE ONCE WAS A TRUE LOVE OF MINE.

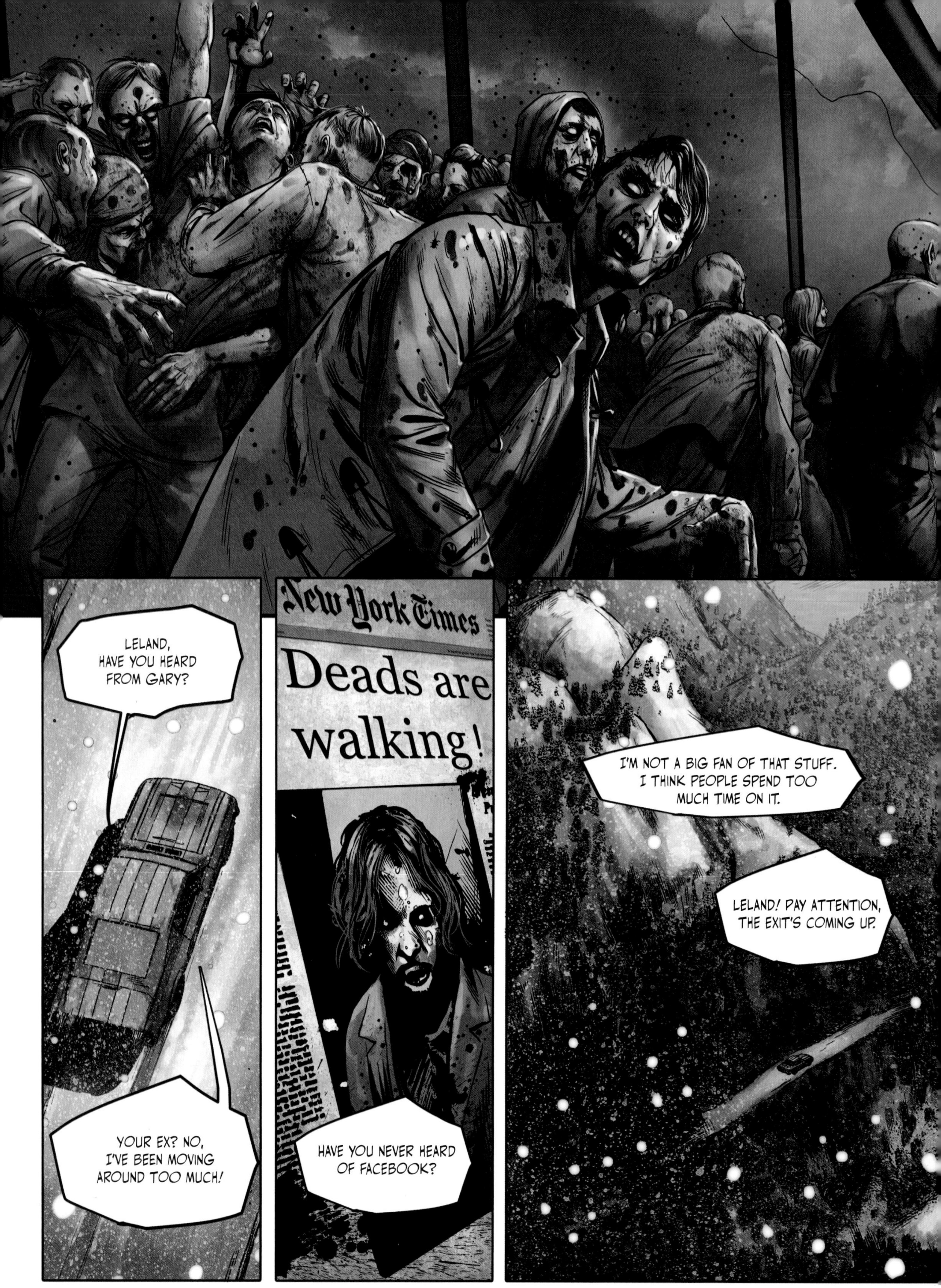
LELAND, HAVE YOU HEARD FROM GARY?
YOUR EX? NO, I'VE BEEN MOVING AROUND TOO MUCH!
New York Times
Deads are walking!
HAVE YOU NEVER HEARD OF FACEBOOK?
I'M NOT A BIG FAN OF THAT STUFF. I THINK PEOPLE SPEND TOO MUCH TIME ON IT.
LELAND! PAY ATTENTION, THE EXIT'S COMING UP.

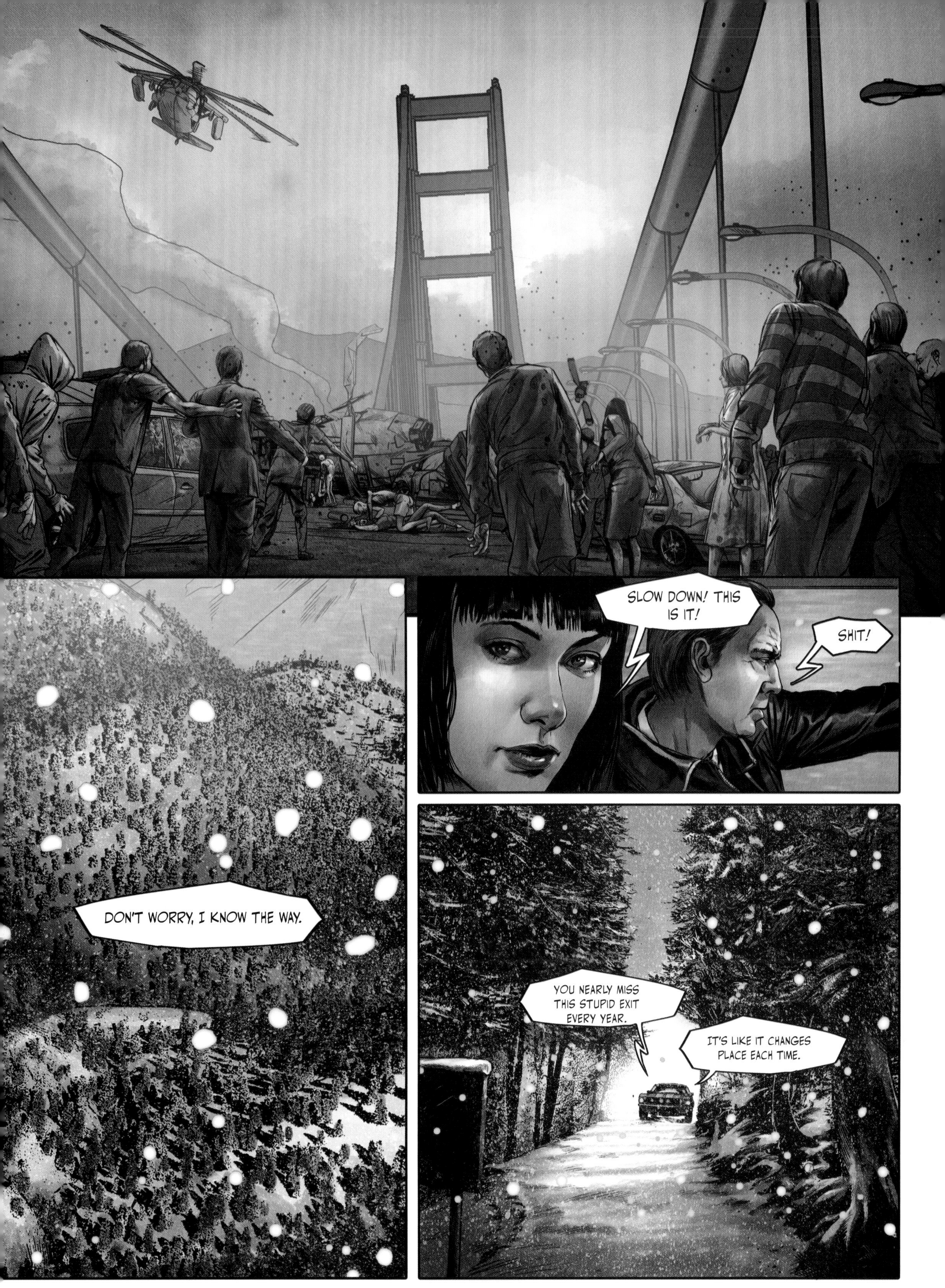
SLOW DOWN! THIS IS IT!
SHIT!
DON'T WORRY, I KNOW THE WAY.
YOU NEARLY MISS THIS STUPID EXIT EVERY YEAR.
IT'S LIKE IT CHANGES PLACE EACH TIME.

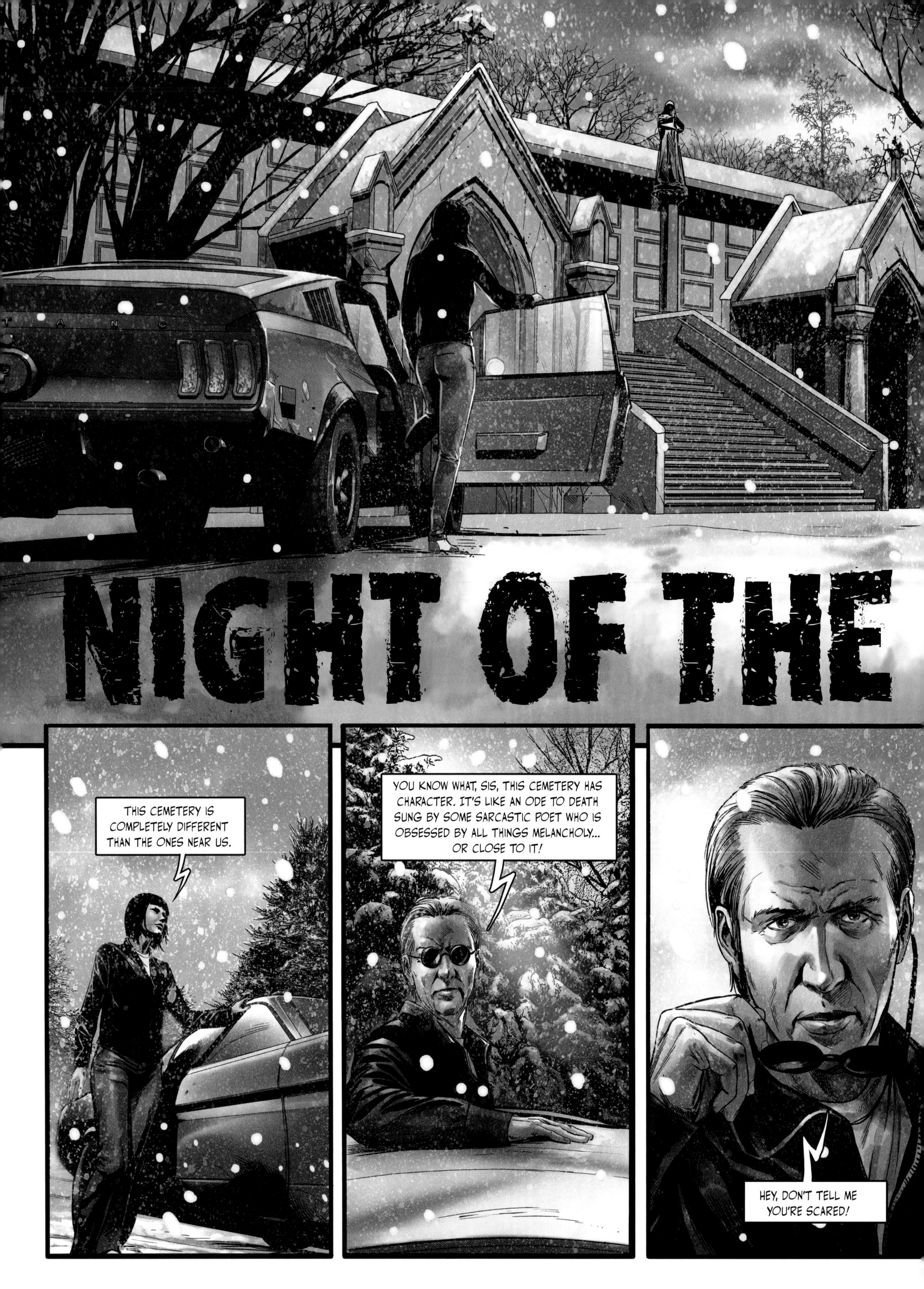
NIGHT OF THE
THIS CEMETERY IS COMPLETELY DIFFERENT THAN THE ONES NEAR US.
YOU KNOW WHAT, SIS, THIS CEMETERY HAS CHARACTER. IT'S LIKE AN ODE TO DEATH SUNG BY SOME SARCASTIC POET WHO IS OBSESSED BY ALL THINGS MELANCHOLY... OR CLOSE TO IT!
HEY, DON'T TELL ME YOU'RE SCARED!

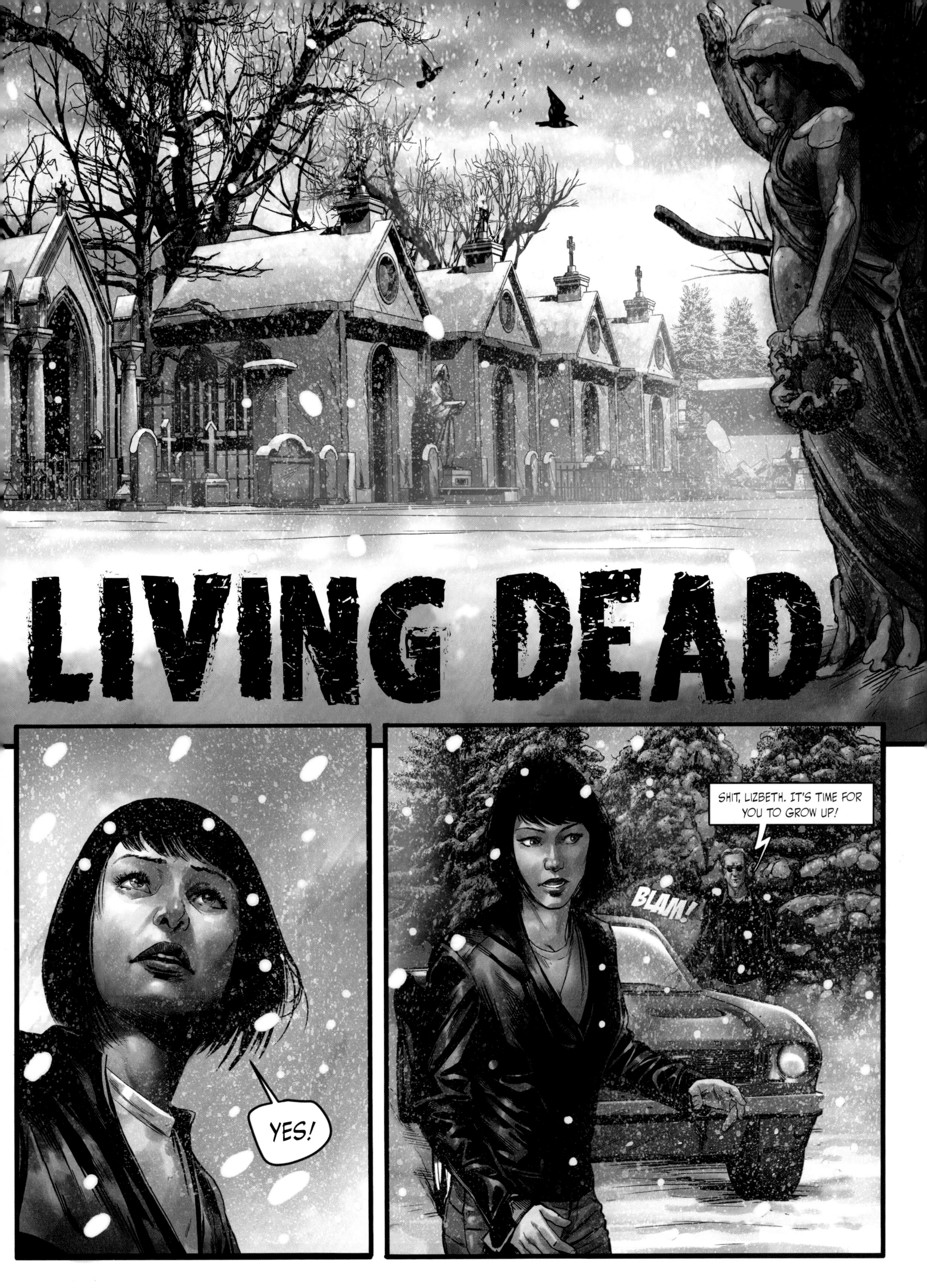
LIVING DEAD
YES!
SHIT, LIZBETH. IT'S TIME FOR YOU TO GROW UP!
BLAM!

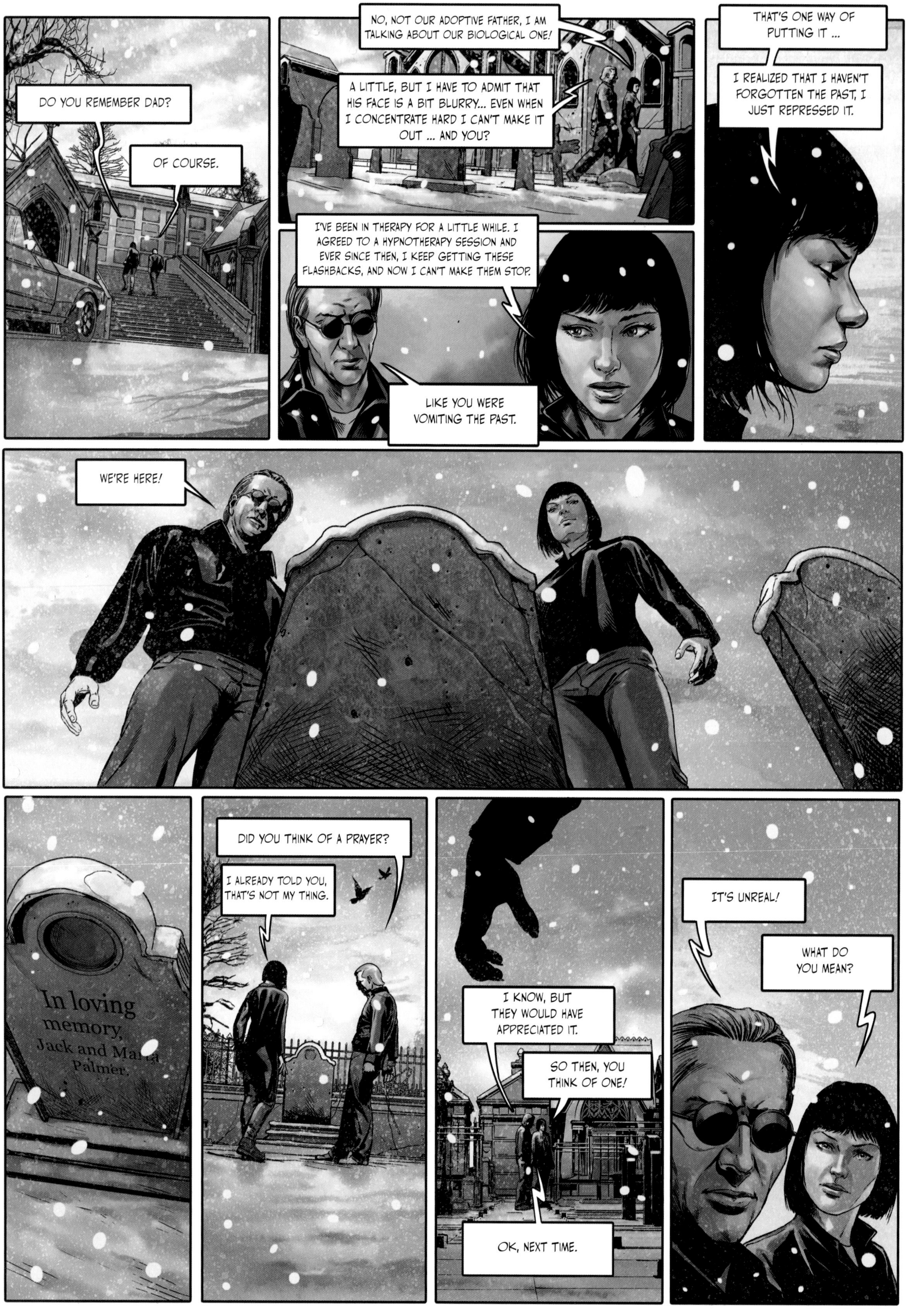
DO YOU REMEMBER DAD?
OF COURSE.
NO, NOT OUR ADOPTIVE FATHER, I AM TALKING ABOUT OUR BIOLOGICAL ONE!
A LITTLE, BUT I HAVE TO ADMIT THAT HIS FACE IS A BIT BLURRY... EVEN WHEN I CONCENTRATE HARD I CAN'T MAKE IT OUT ... AND YOU?
I'VE BEEN IN THERAPY FOR A LITTLE WHILE. I AGREED TO A HYPNOTHERAPY SESSION AND EVER SINCE THEN, I KEEP GETTING THESE FLASHBACKS, AND NOW I CAN'T MAKE THEM STOP.
LIKE YOU WERE VOMITING THE PAST.
THAT'S ONE WAY OF PUTTING IT ...
I REALIZED THAT I HAVEN'T FORGOTTEN THE PAST, I JUST REPRESSED IT.
WE'RE HERE!
In loving memory, Jack and Maria Palmer.
DID YOU THINK OF A PRAYER?
I ALREADY TOLD YOU, THAT'S NOT MY THING.
I KNOW, BUT THEY WOULD HAVE APPRECIATED IT.
SO THEN, YOU THINK OF ONE!
OK, NEXT TIME.
IT'S UNREAL!
WHAT DO YOU MEAN?

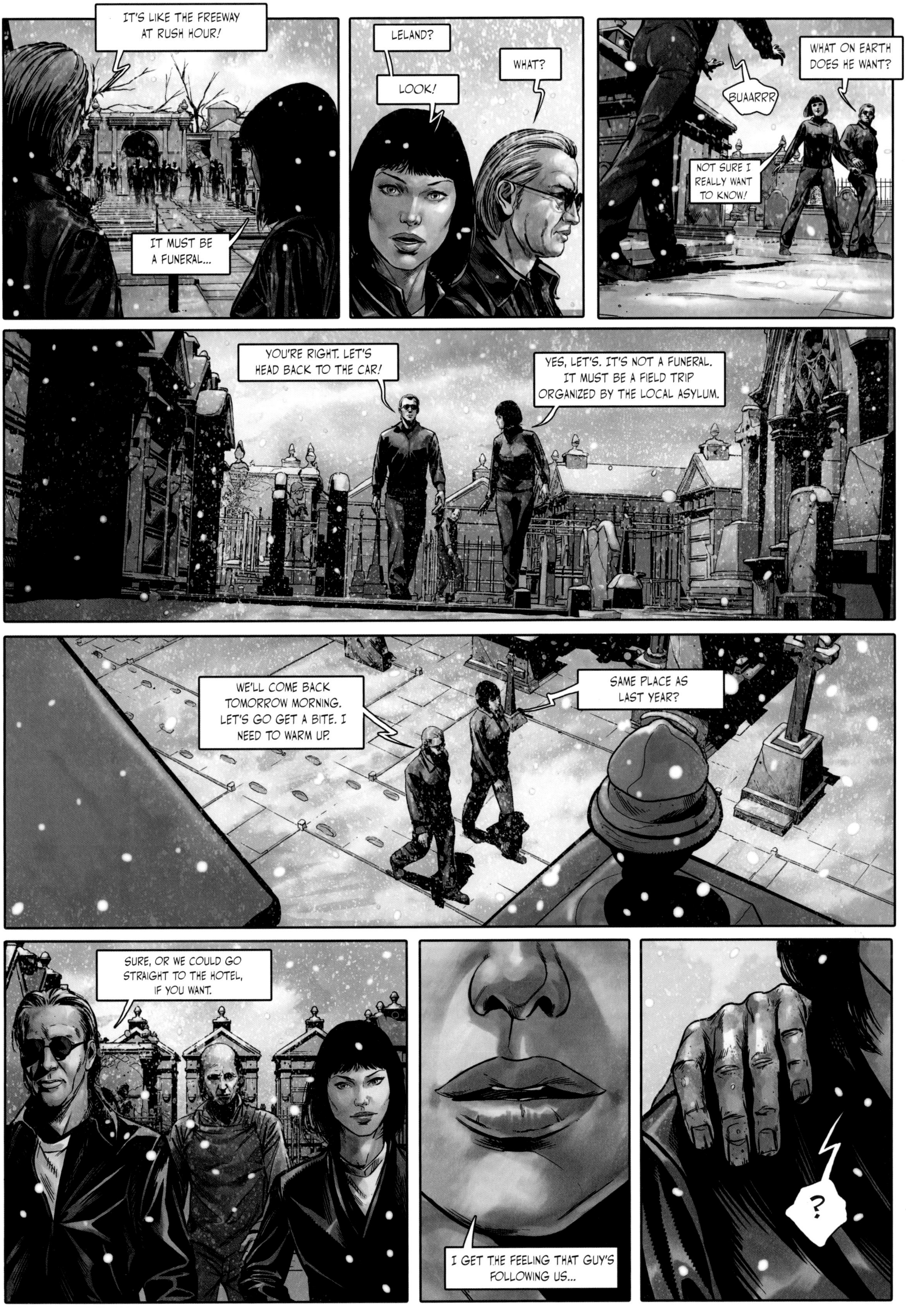
IT'S LIKE THE FREEWAY AT RUSH HOUR!
IT MUST BE A FUNERAL...
LELAND?
LOOK!
WHAT?
BUAARRR
WHAT ON EARTH DOES HE WANT?
NOT SURE I REALLY WANT TO KNOW!
YOU'RE RIGHT. LET'S HEAD BACK TO THE CAR!
YES, LET'S. IT'S NOT A FUNERAL. IT MUST BE A FIELD TRIP ORGANIZED BY THE LOCAL ASYLUM.
WE'LL COME BACK TOMORROW MORNING. LET'S GO GET A BITE. I NEED TO WARM UP.
SAME PLACE AS LAST YEAR?
SURE, OR WE COULD GO STRAIGHT TO THE HOTEL, IF YOU WANT.
I GET THE FEELING THAT GUY'S FOLLOWING US...
?

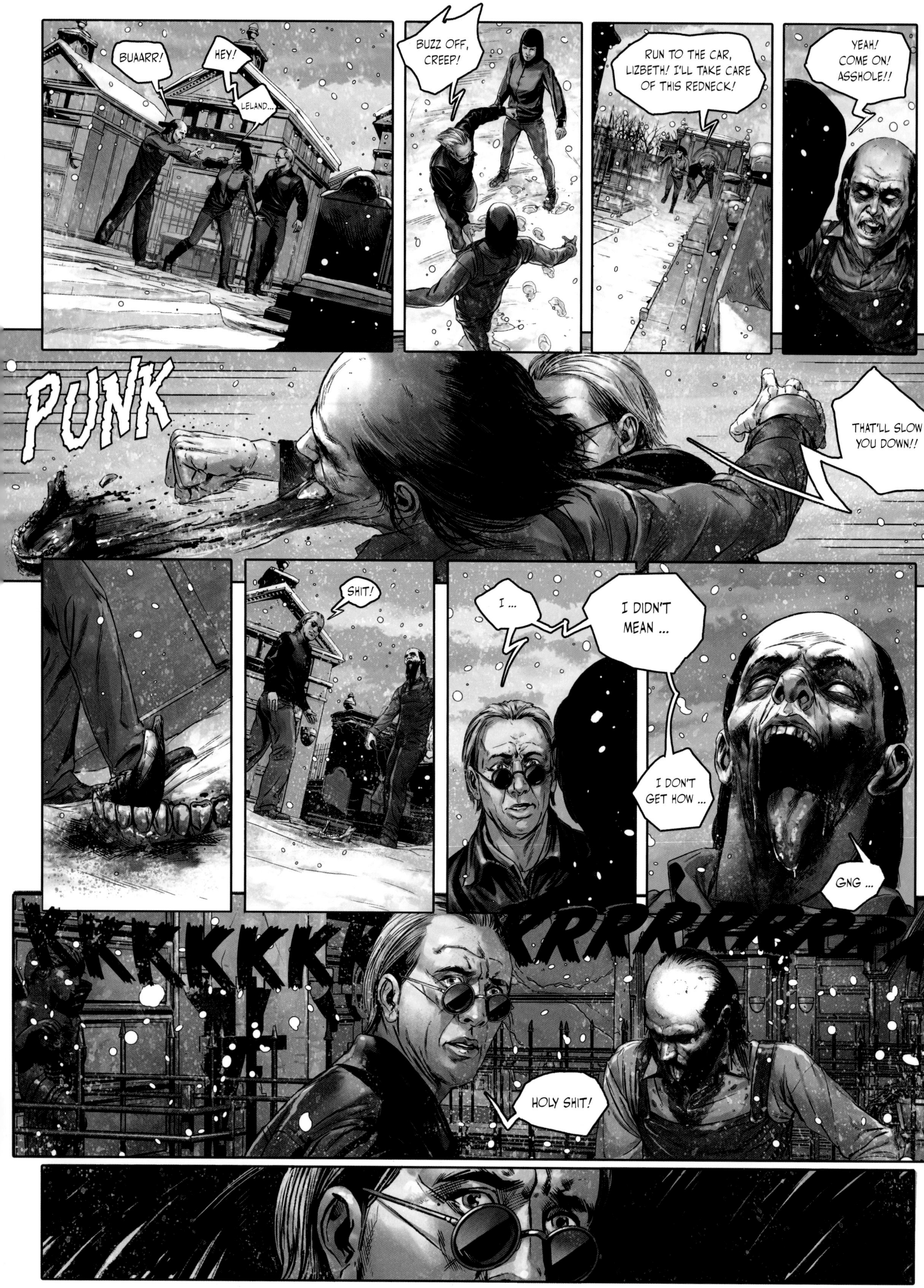
BUAARR!
HEY!
LELAND...
BUZZ OFF, CREEP!
RUN TO THE CAR, LIZBETH! I'LL TAKE CARE OF THIS REDNECK!
YEAH! COME ON! ASSHOLE!!
PUNK
THAT'LL SLOW YOU DOWN!!
SHIT!
I ...
I DIDN'T MEAN ...
I DON'T GET HOW ...
GNG ...
KKKKKKRRRRRRRRR
HOLY SHIT!

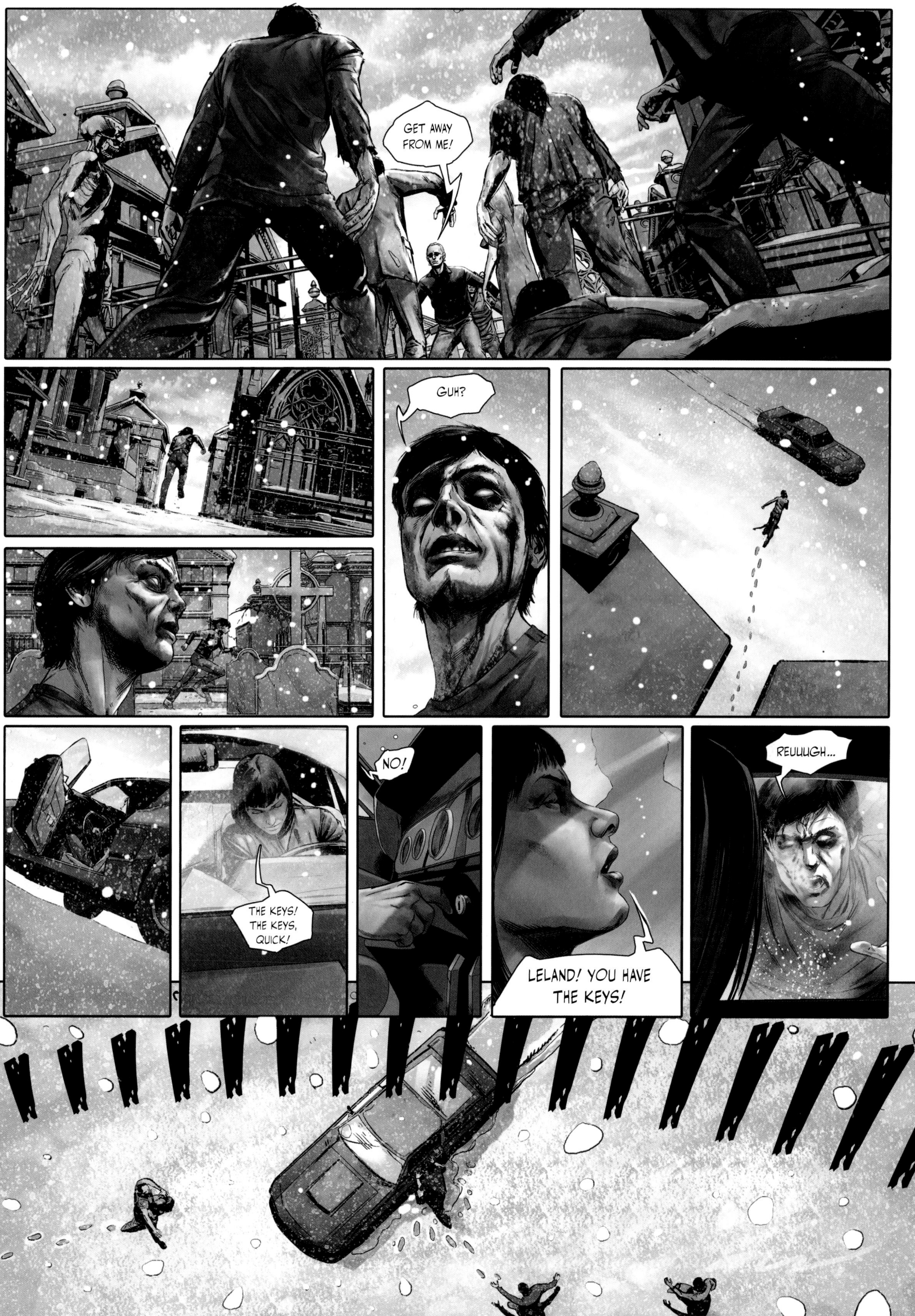
GET AWAY FROM ME!
GUH?
NO!
THE KEYS! THE KEYS, QUICK!
LELAND! YOU HAVE THE KEYS!
REUUUGH...

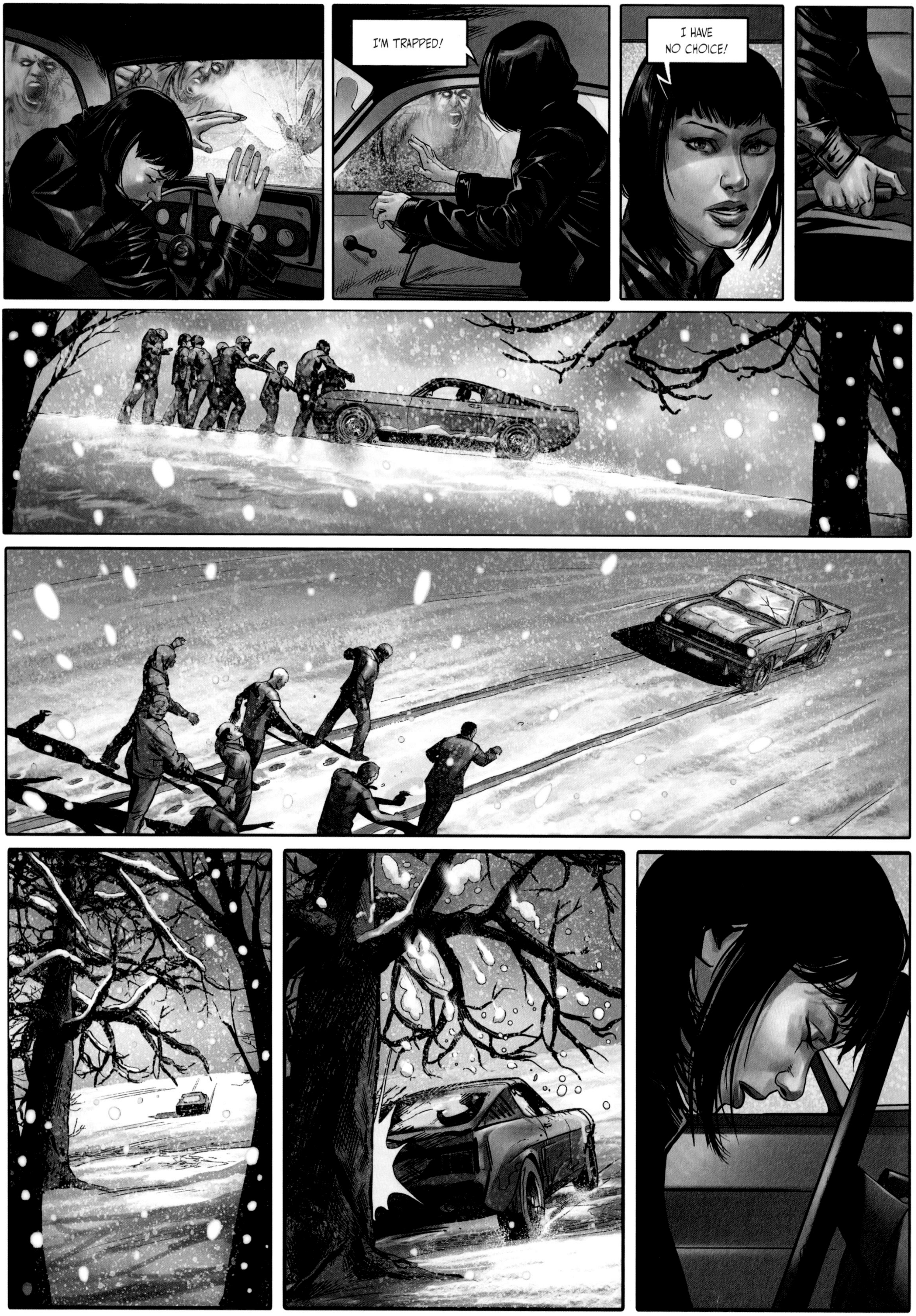
I'M TRAPPED!
I HAVE NO CHOICE!

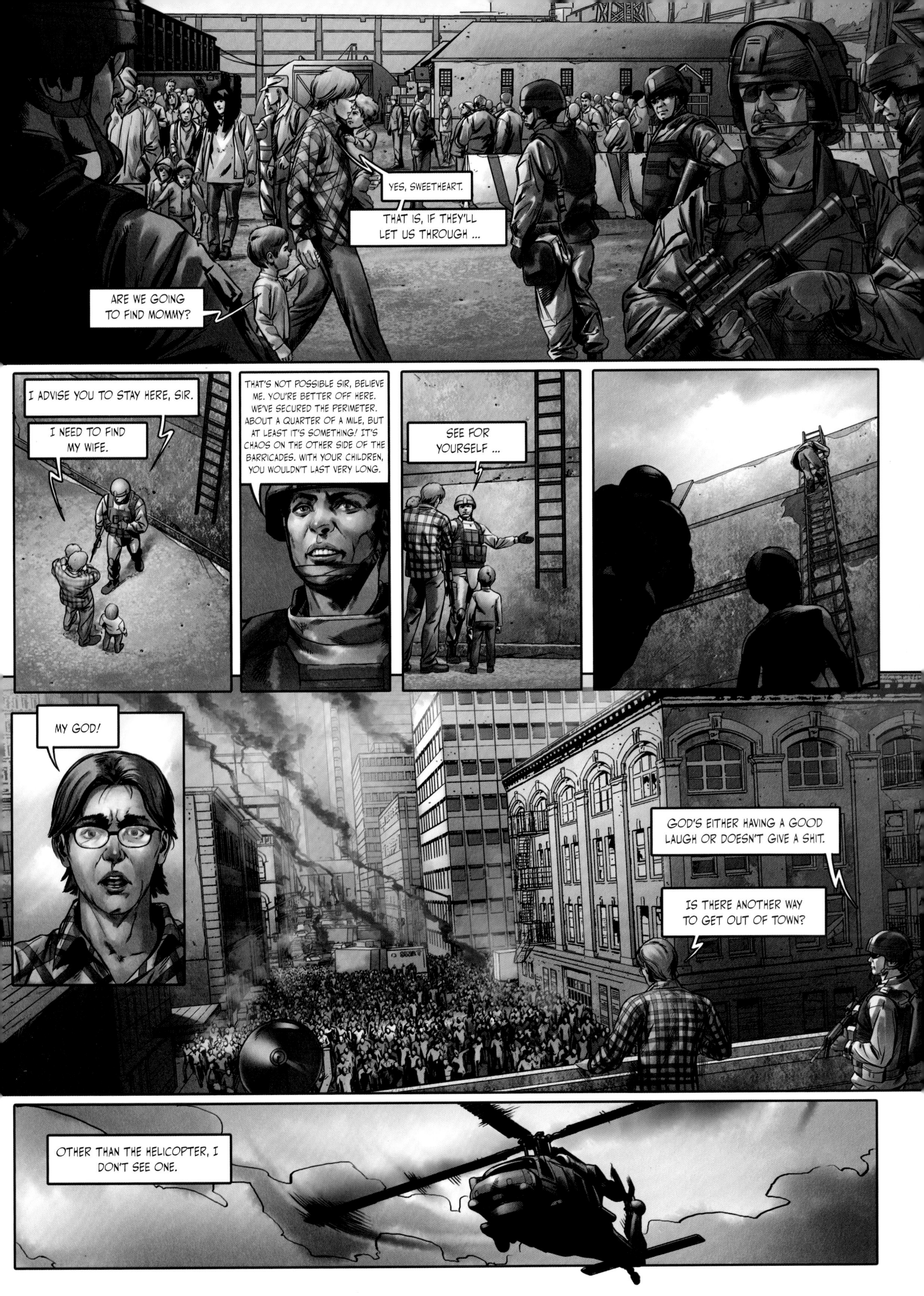
YES, SWEETHEART.
THAT IS, IF THEY'LL LET US THROUGH ...
ARE WE GOING TO FIND MOMMY?
I ADVISE YOU TO STAY HERE, SIR.
I NEED TO FIND MY WIFE.
THAT'S NOT POSSIBLE SIR, BELIEVE ME. YOU'RE BETTER OFF HERE. WE'VE SECURED THE PERIMETER. ABOUT A QUARTER OF A MILE, BUT AT LEAST IT'S SOMETHING! IT'S CHAOS ON THE OTHER SIDE OF THE BARRICADES. WITH YOUR CHILDREN, YOU WOULDN'T LAST VERY LONG.
SEE FOR YOURSELF ...
MY GOD!
GOD'S EITHER HAVING A GOOD LAUGH OR DOESN'T GIVE A SHIT.
IS THERE ANOTHER WAY TO GET OUT OF TOWN?
OTHER THAN THE HELICOPTER, I DON'T SEE ONE.

I'LL START THE COUNT ...

AT THE END, YOU'LL BE ASLEEP ...

5 ...

3 ...

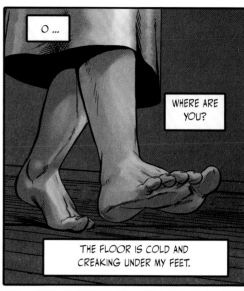

0 ...

WHERE ARE YOU?

THE FLOOR IS COLD AND CREAKING UNDER MY FEET.

I'M IN OUR OLD HOUSE.

YOU'RE NOT WEARING SLIPPERS?

NO, I AM TRYING TO BE AS QUIET AS I CAN.

I DON'T KNOW WHAT I AM DOING THERE, BUT IT'S THE MIDDLE OF THE NIGHT.

I AM HEADING FOR THE BASEMENT DOOR. THERE'S A LIGHT ON.

I WANT TO KNOW ...

EVERY NIGHT I WOULD HEAR NOISES COMING FROM THE BASEMENT AND MY FATHER FORBADE ME TO GO DOWN THERE.

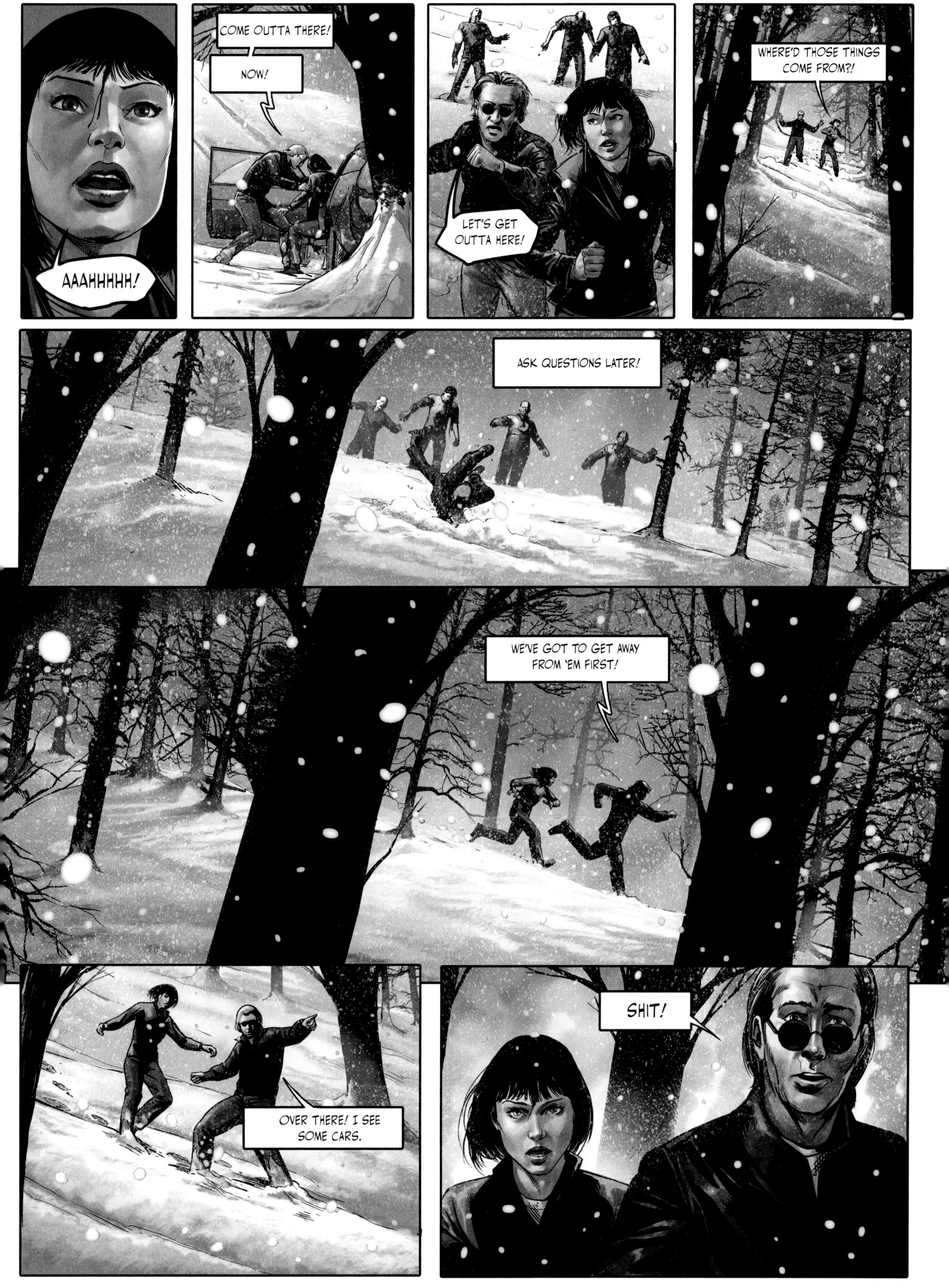
AAAHHHHH!
COME OUTTA THERE!
NOW!
LET'S GET OUTTA HERE!
WHERE'D THOSE THINGS COME FROM?!
ASK QUESTIONS LATER!
WE'VE GOT TO GET AWAY FROM 'EM FIRST!
OVER THERE! I SEE SOME CARS.
SHIT!

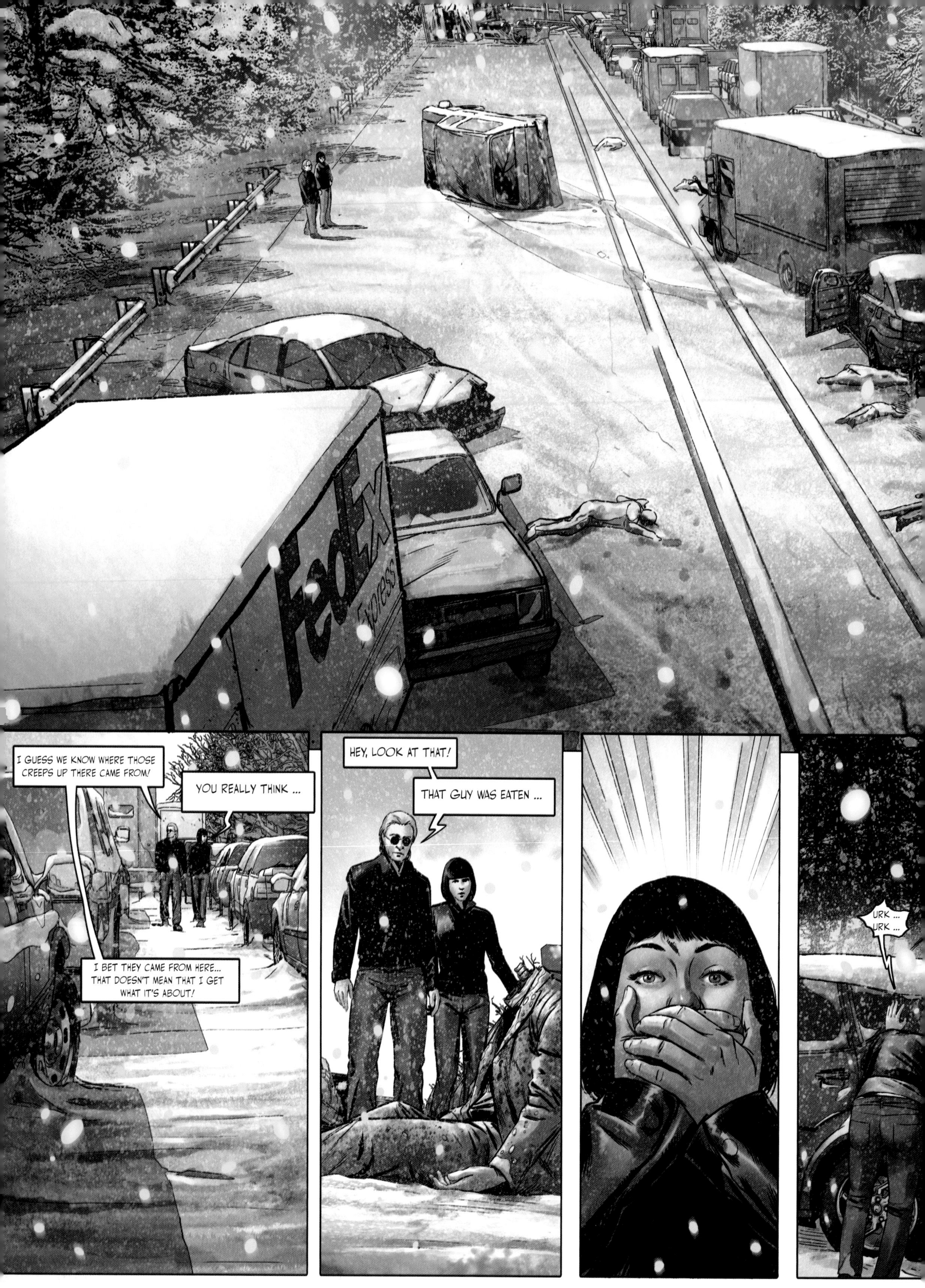
I GUESS WE KNOW WHERE THOSE CREEPS UP THERE CAME FROM!
YOU REALLY THINK ...
I BET THEY CAME FROM HERE... THAT DOESN'T MEAN THAT I GET WHAT IT'S ABOUT!
HEY, LOOK AT THAT!
THAT GUY WAS EATEN ...
URK ... URK ...

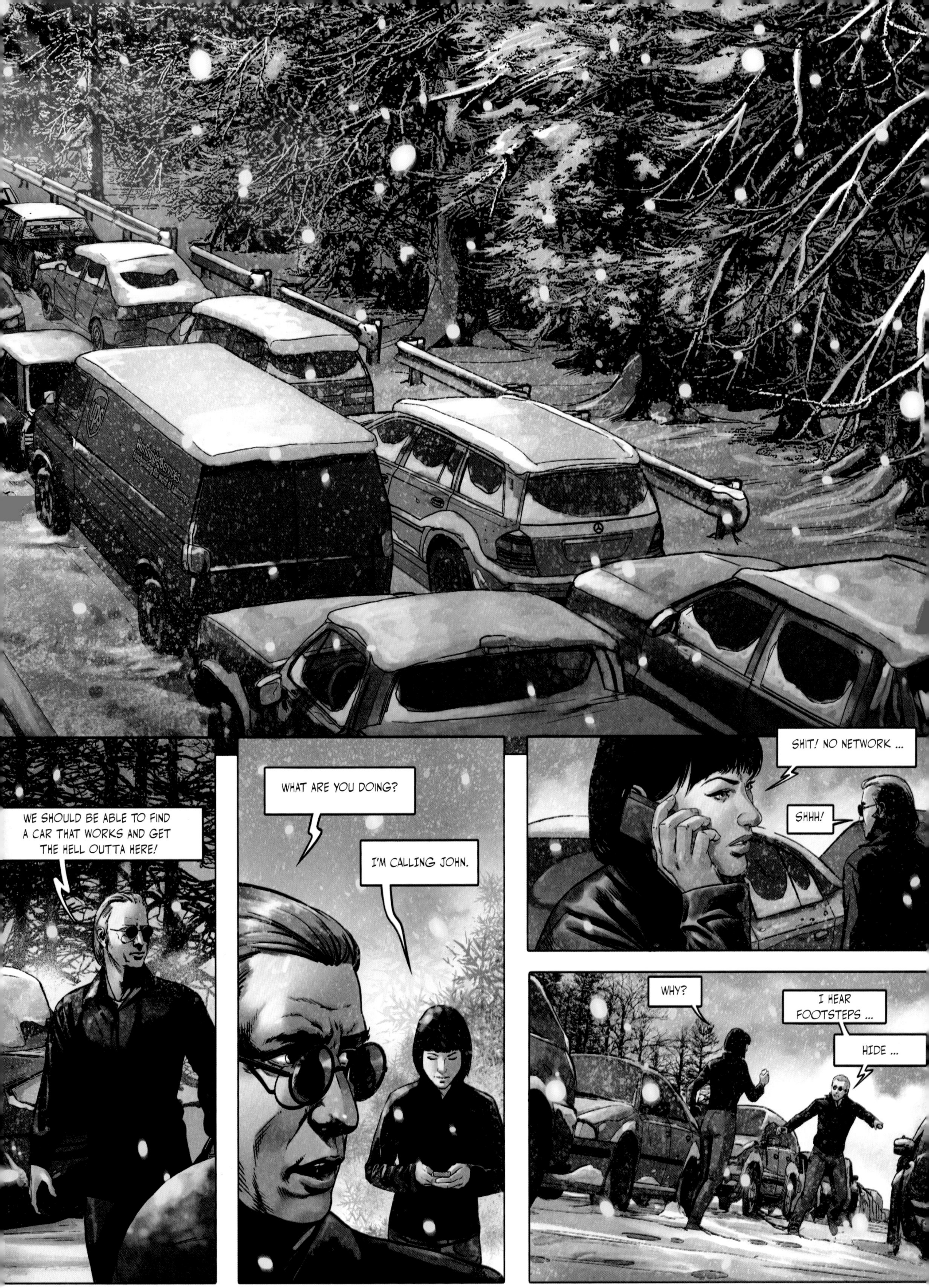
WE SHOULD BE ABLE TO FIND A CAR THAT WORKS AND GET THE HELL OUTTA HERE!
WHAT ARE YOU DOING?
I'M CALLING JOHN.
SHIT! NO NETWORK ...
SHHH!
WHY?
I HEAR FOOTSTEPS ...
HIDE ...

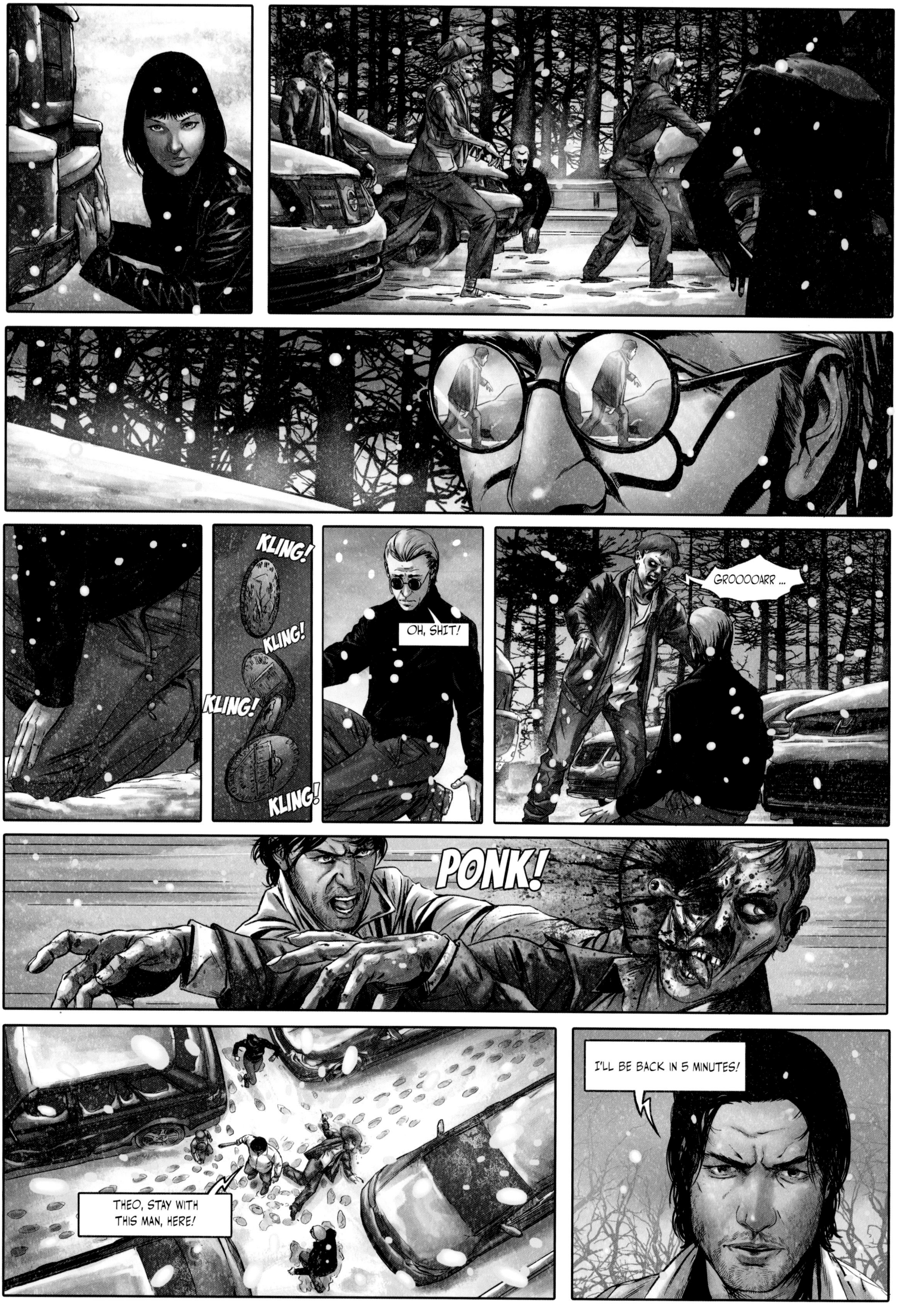
KLING!
KLING!
KLING!
KLING!
OH, SHIT!
GROOOOARR ...
PONK!
THEO, STAY WITH THIS MAN, HERE!
I'LL BE BACK IN 5 MINUTES!

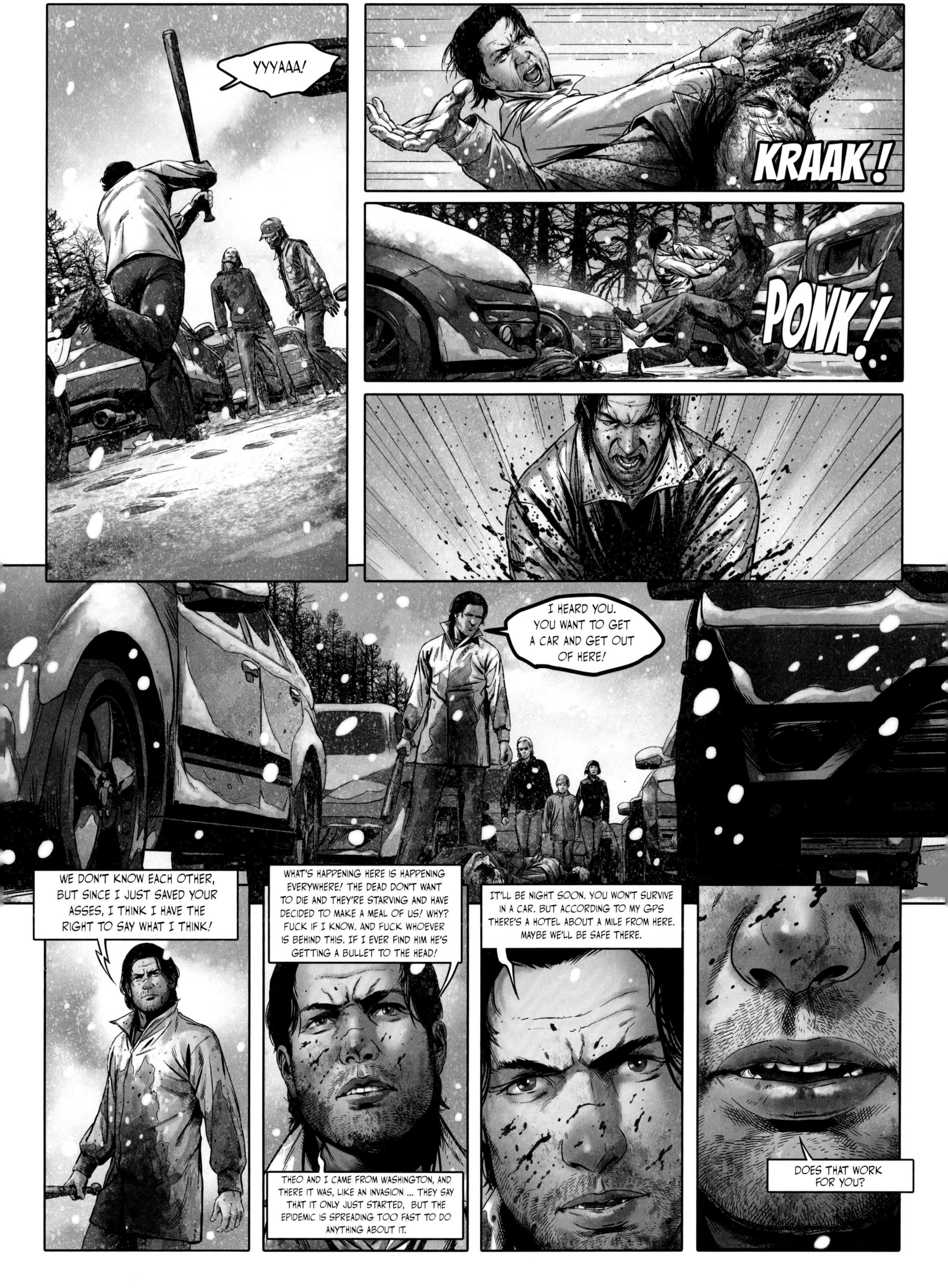
YYYAAA!
KRAAK!
PONK!
I HEARD YOU. YOU WANT TO GET A CAR AND GET OUT OF HERE!
WE DON'T KNOW EACH OTHER, BUT SINCE I JUST SAVED YOUR ASSES, I THINK I HAVE THE RIGHT TO SAY WHAT I THINK!
WHAT'S HAPPENING HERE IS HAPPENING EVERYWHERE! THE DEAD DON'T WANT TO DIE AND THEY'RE STARVING AND HAVE DECIDED TO MAKE A MEAL OF US! WHY? FUCK IF I KNOW. AND FUCK WHOEVER IS BEHIND THIS. IF I EVER FIND HIM HE'S GETTING A BULLET TO THE HEAD!
THEO AND I CAME FROM WASHINGTON, AND THERE IT WAS, LIKE AN INVASION ... THEY SAY THAT IT ONLY JUST STARTED, BUT THE EPIDEMIC IS SPREADING TOO FAST TO DO ANYTHING ABOUT IT.
IT'LL BE NIGHT SOON. YOU WON'T SURVIVE IN A CAR. BUT ACCORDING TO MY GPS THERE'S A HOTEL ABOUT A MILE FROM HERE. MAYBE WE'LL BE SAFE THERE.
DOES THAT WORK FOR YOU?

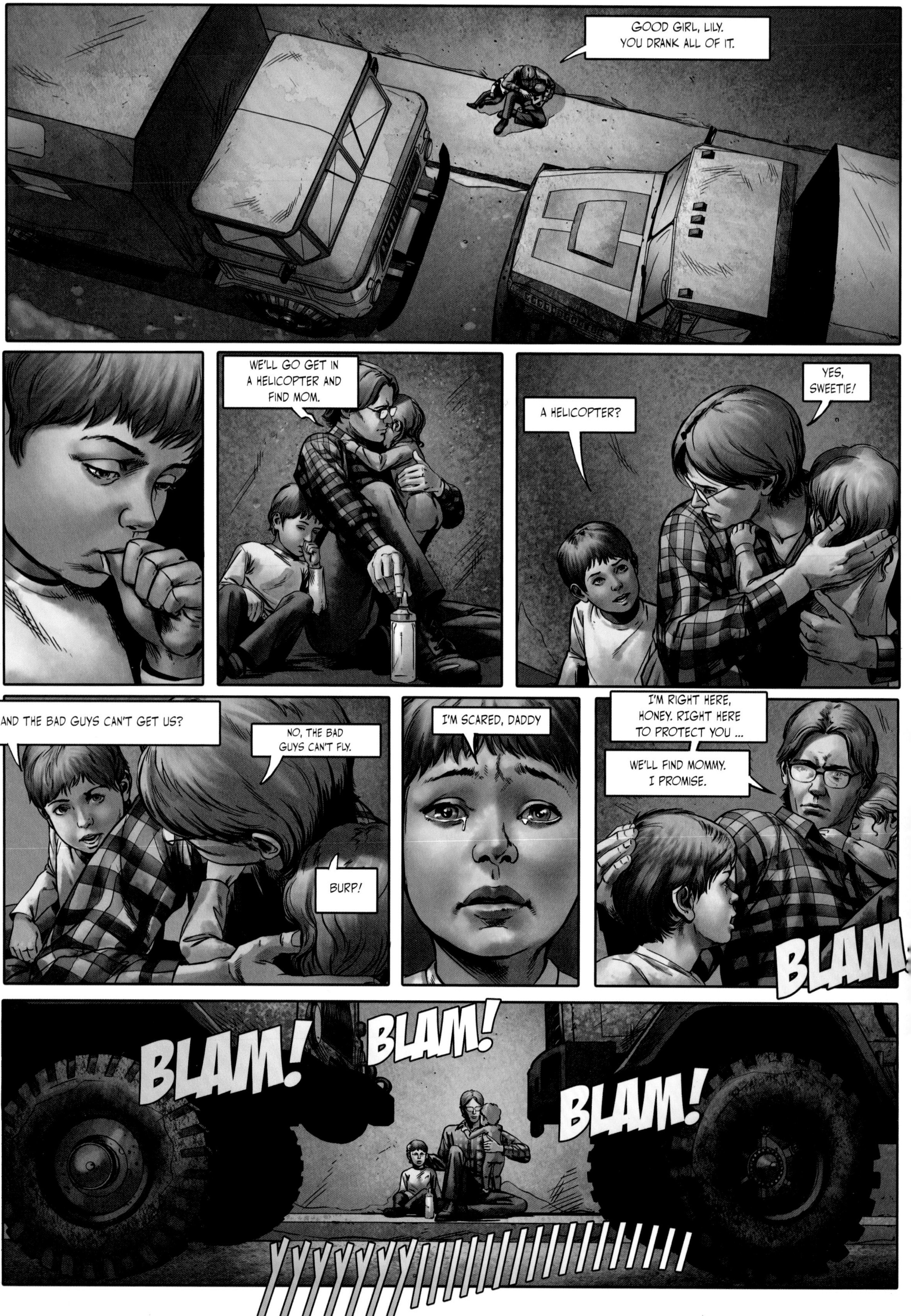
GOOD GIRL, LILY. YOU DRANK ALL OF IT.
WE'LL GO GET IN A HELICOPTER AND FIND MOM.
A HELICOPTER?
YES, SWEETIE!
AND THE BAD GUYS CAN'T GET US?
NO, THE BAD GUYS CAN'T FLY.
BURP!
I'M SCARED, DADDY
I'M RIGHT HERE, HONEY. RIGHT HERE TO PROTECT YOU ...
WE'LL FIND MOMMY. I PROMISE.
BLAM!
BLAM!
BLAM!
BLAM!
YYYYYYYIIIIIIIIIIIIIIIIIIIIIII

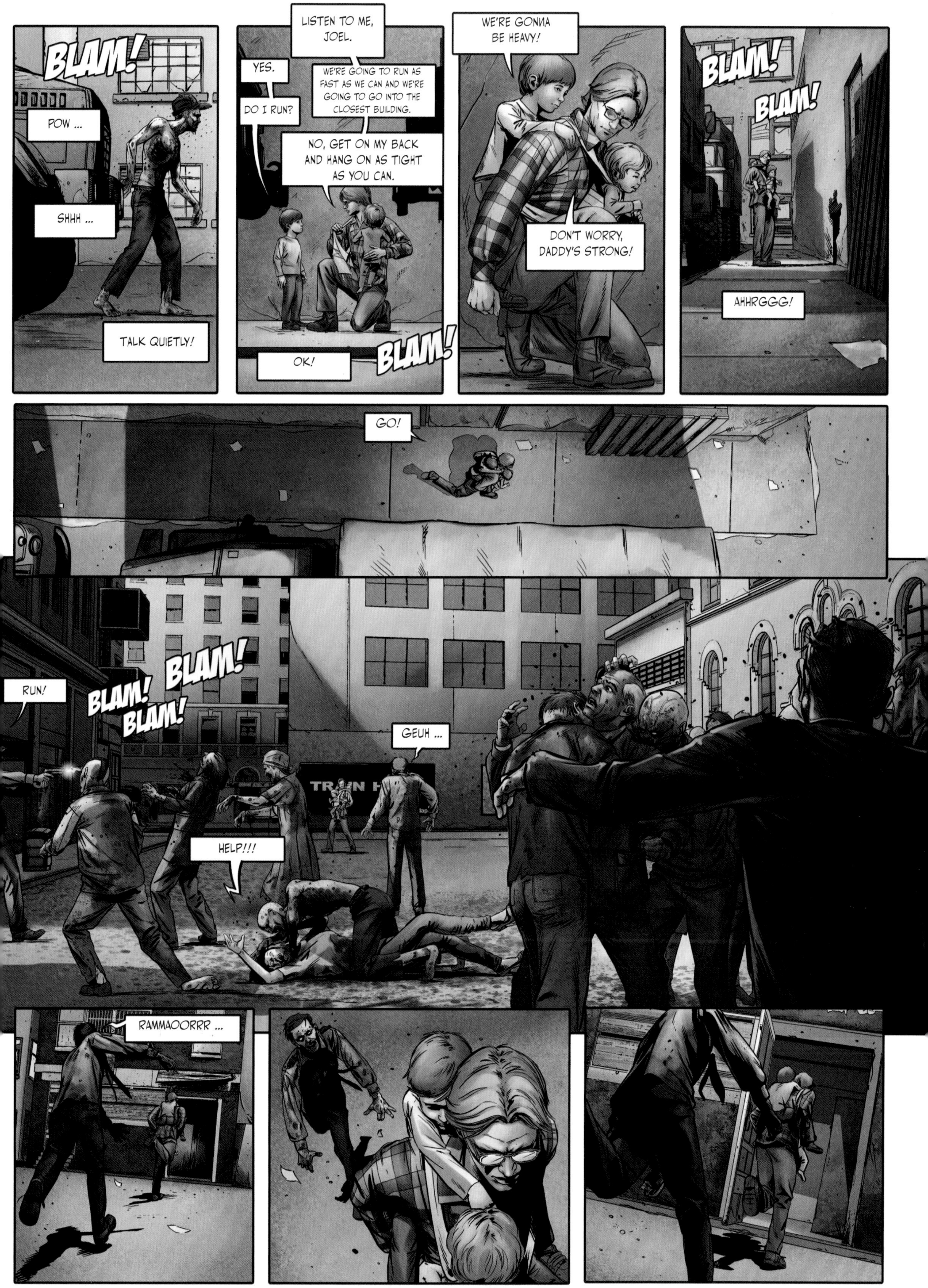
BLAM!
POW ...
SHHH ...
TALK QUIETLY!
LISTEN TO ME, JOEL.
YES.
DO I RUN?
WE'RE GOING TO RUN AS FAST AS WE CAN AND WE'RE GOING TO GO INTO THE CLOSEST BUILDING.
NO, GET ON MY BACK AND HANG ON AS TIGHT AS YOU CAN.
OK!
BLAM!
WE'RE GONNA BE HEAVY!
DON'T WORRY, DADDY'S STRONG!
BLAM!
BLAM!
AHHRGGG!
GO!
RUN!
BLAM!
BLAM!
BLAM!
GEUH ...
HELP!!!
RAMMAOORRR ...

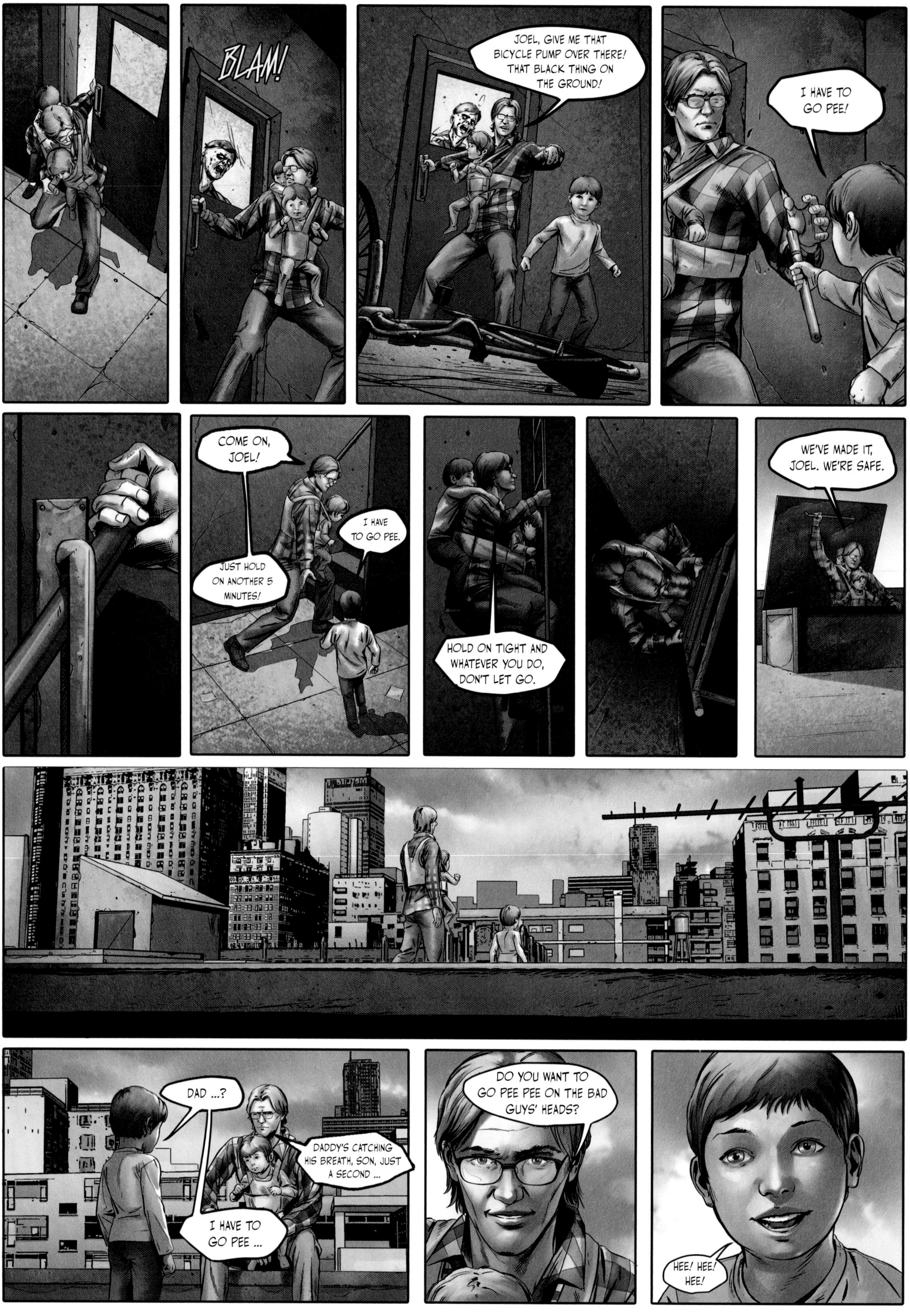

BLAM!
JOEL, GIVE ME THAT BICYCLE PUMP OVER THERE! THAT BLACK THING ON THE GROUND!
I HAVE TO GO PEE!
COME ON, JOEL!
JUST HOLD ON ANOTHER 5 MINUTES!
I HAVE TO GO PEE.
HOLD ON TIGHT AND WHATEVER YOU DO, DON'T LET GO.
WE'VE MADE IT, JOEL. WE'RE SAFE.
DAD ...?
DADDY'S CATCHING HIS BREATH, SON, JUST A SECOND ...
I HAVE TO GO PEE ...
DO YOU WANT TO GO PEE PEE ON THE BAD GUYS' HEADS?
HEE! HEE! HEE!

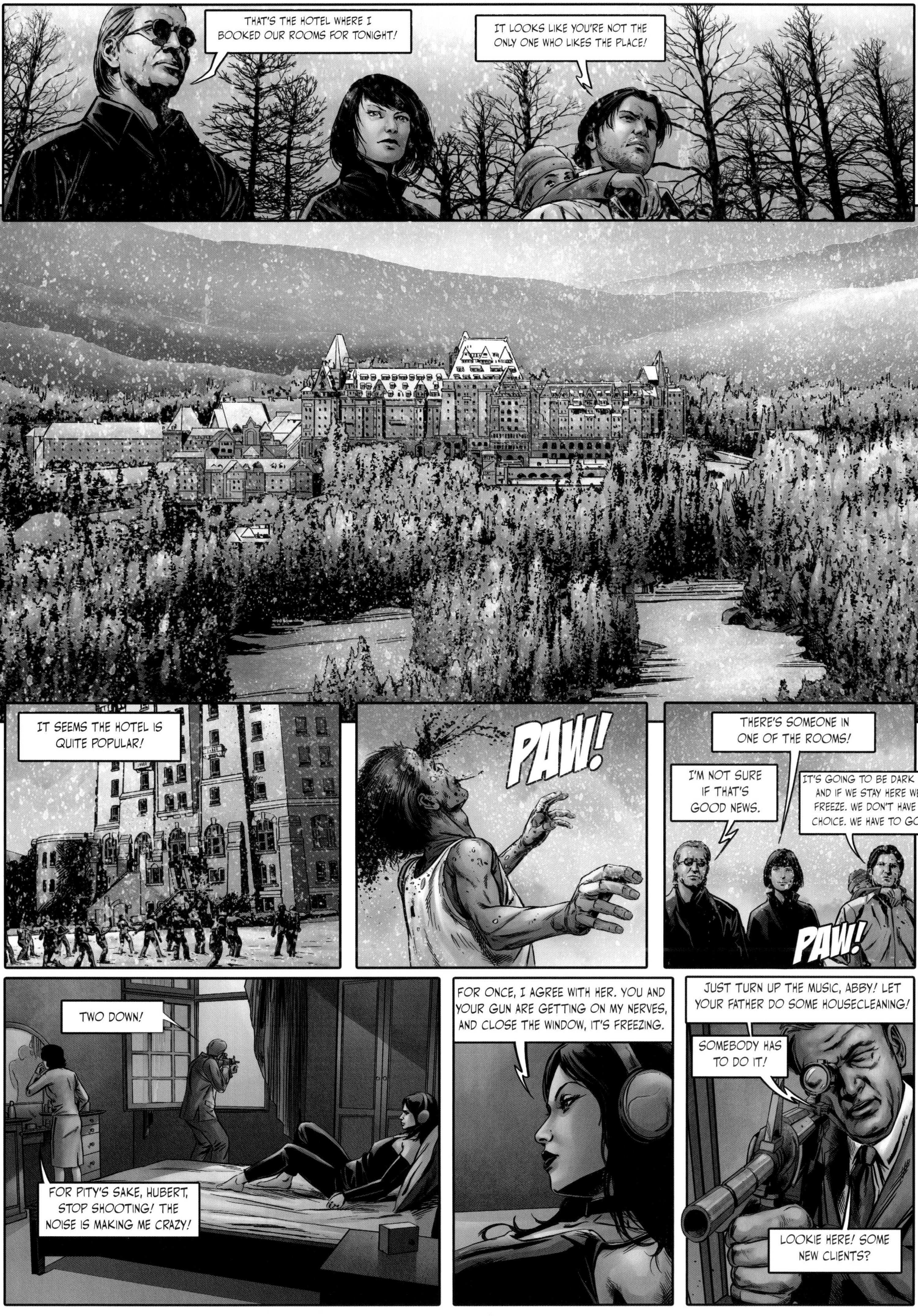
THAT'S THE HOTEL WHERE I BOOKED OUR ROOMS FOR TONIGHT!
IT LOOKS LIKE YOU'RE NOT THE ONLY ONE WHO LIKES THE PLACE!
IT SEEMS THE HOTEL IS QUITE POPULAR!
PAW!
THERE'S SOMEONE IN ONE OF THE ROOMS!
I'M NOT SURE IF THAT'S GOOD NEWS.
IT'S GOING TO BE DARK SOON, AND IF WE STAY HERE WE'LL FREEZE. WE DON'T HAVE ANY CHOICE. WE HAVE TO GO IN!
PAW!
TWO DOWN!
FOR PITY'S SAKE, HUBERT, STOP SHOOTING! THE NOISE IS MAKING ME CRAZY!
FOR ONCE, I AGREE WITH HER. YOU AND YOUR GUN ARE GETTING ON MY NERVES, AND CLOSE THE WINDOW, IT'S FREEZING.
JUST TURN UP THE MUSIC, ABBY! LET YOUR FATHER DO SOME HOUSECLEANING!
SOMEBODY HAS TO DO IT!
LOOKIE HERE! SOME NEW CLIENTS?

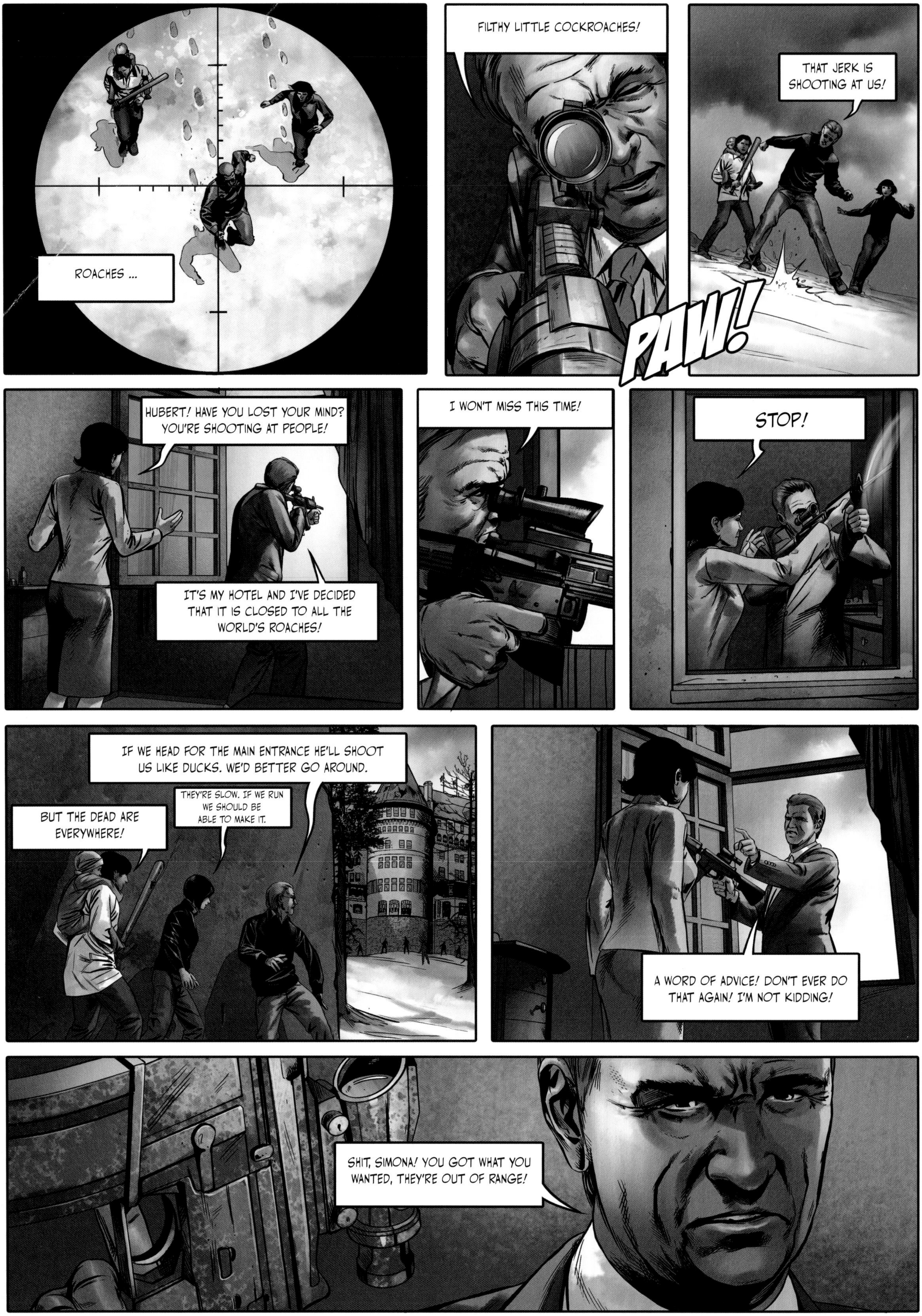
ROACHES ...
FILTHY LITTLE COCKROACHES!
THAT JERK IS SHOOTING AT US!
PAW!
HUBERT! HAVE YOU LOST YOUR MIND? YOU'RE SHOOTING AT PEOPLE!
IT'S MY HOTEL AND I'VE DECIDED THAT IT IS CLOSED TO ALL THE WORLD'S ROACHES!
I WON'T MISS THIS TIME!
STOP!
IF WE HEAD FOR THE MAIN ENTRANCE HE'LL SHOOT US LIKE DUCKS. WE'D BETTER GO AROUND.
BUT THE DEAD ARE EVERYWHERE!
THEY'RE SLOW. IF WE RUN WE SHOULD BE ABLE TO MAKE IT.
A WORD OF ADVICE! DON'T EVER DO THAT AGAIN! I'M NOT KIDDING!
SHIT, SIMONA! YOU GOT WHAT YOU WANTED, THEY'RE OUT OF RANGE!

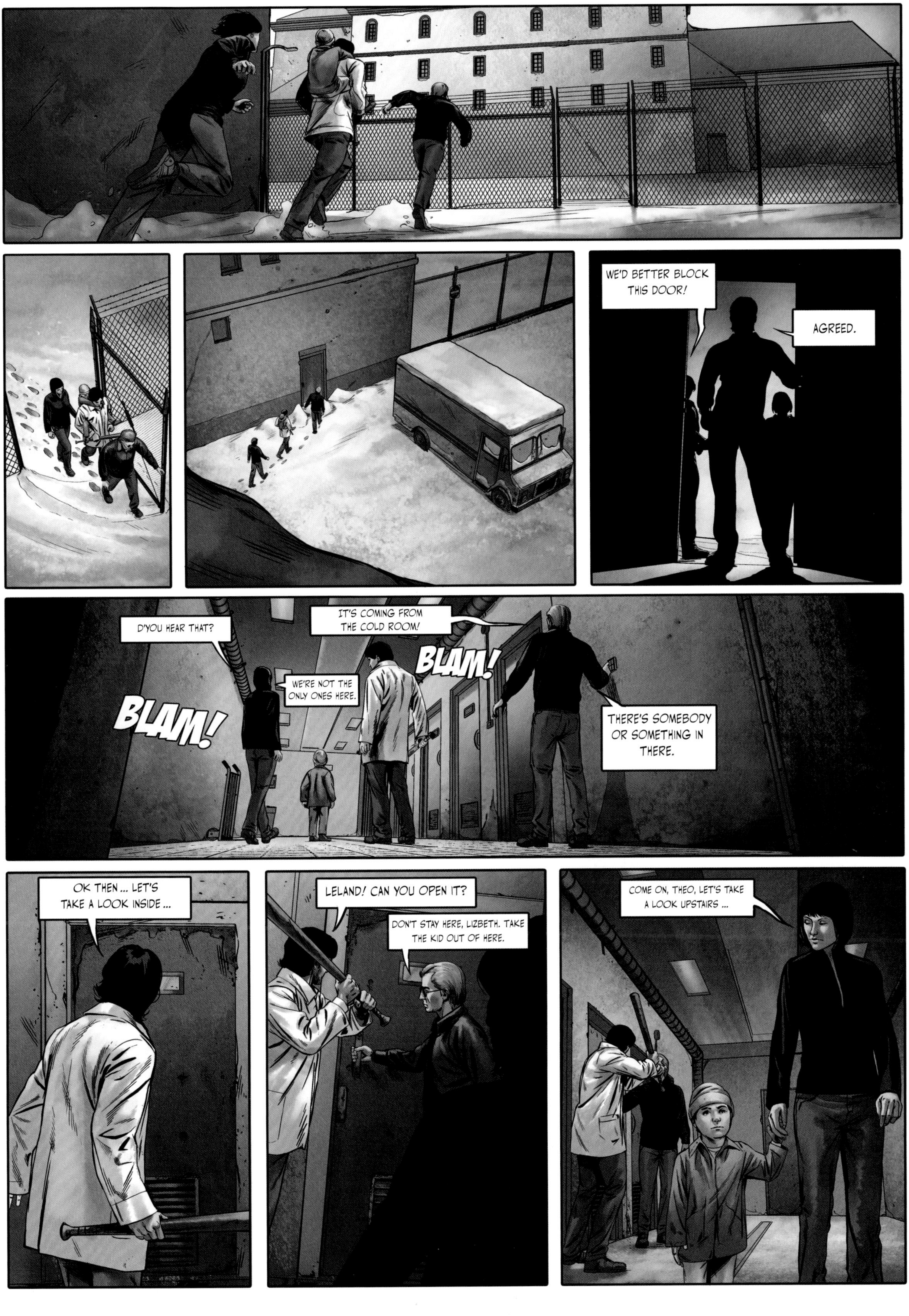
WE'D BETTER BLOCK THIS DOOR!
AGREED.
D'YOU HEAR THAT?
IT'S COMING FROM THE COLD ROOM!
WE'RE NOT THE ONLY ONES HERE.
BLAM!
BLAM!
THERE'S SOMEBODY OR SOMETHING IN THERE.
OK THEN ... LET'S TAKE A LOOK INSIDE ...
LELAND! CAN YOU OPEN IT?
DON'T STAY HERE, LIZBETH. TAKE THE KID OUT OF HERE.
COME ON, THEO, LET'S TAKE A LOOK UPSTAIRS ...

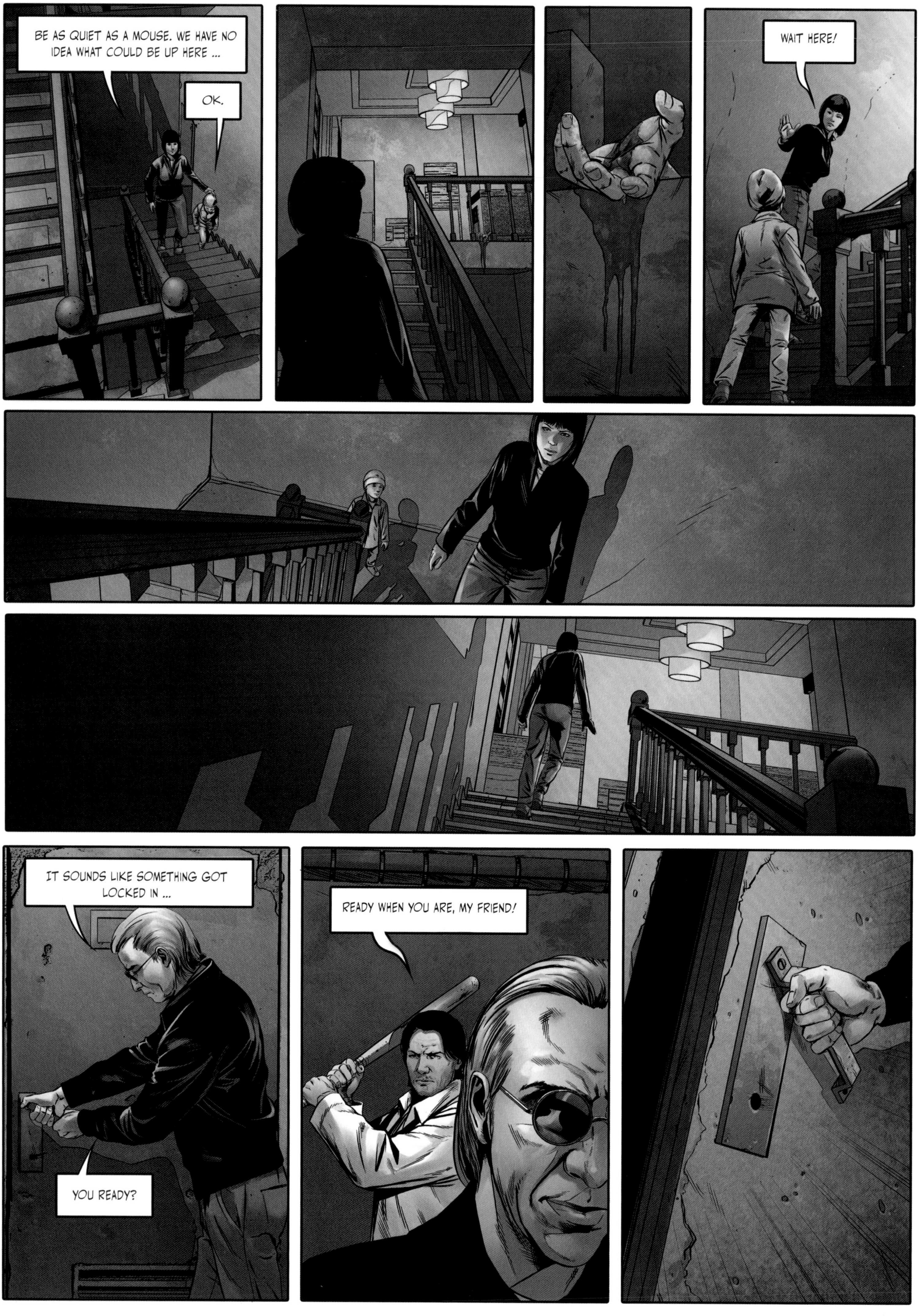
BE AS QUIET AS A MOUSE. WE HAVE NO IDEA WHAT COULD BE UP HERE ...
OK.
WAIT HERE!
IT SOUNDS LIKE SOMETHING GOT LOCKED IN ...
YOU READY?
READY WHEN YOU ARE, MY FRIEND!

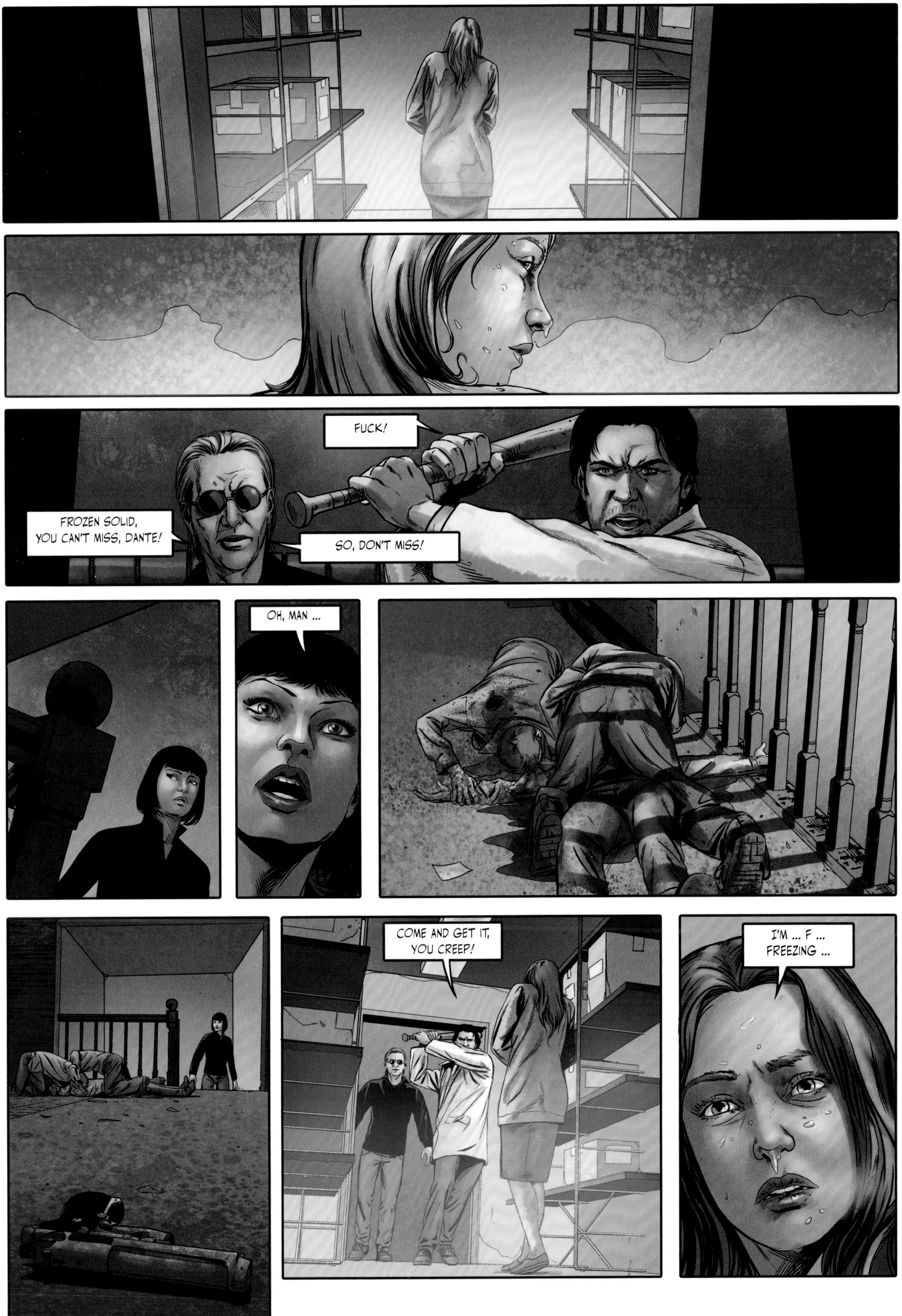
FUCK!
FROZEN SOLID, YOU CAN'T MISS, DANTE!
SO, DON'T MISS!
OH, MAN ...
COME AND GET IT, YOU CREEP!
I'M ... F ... FREEZING ...

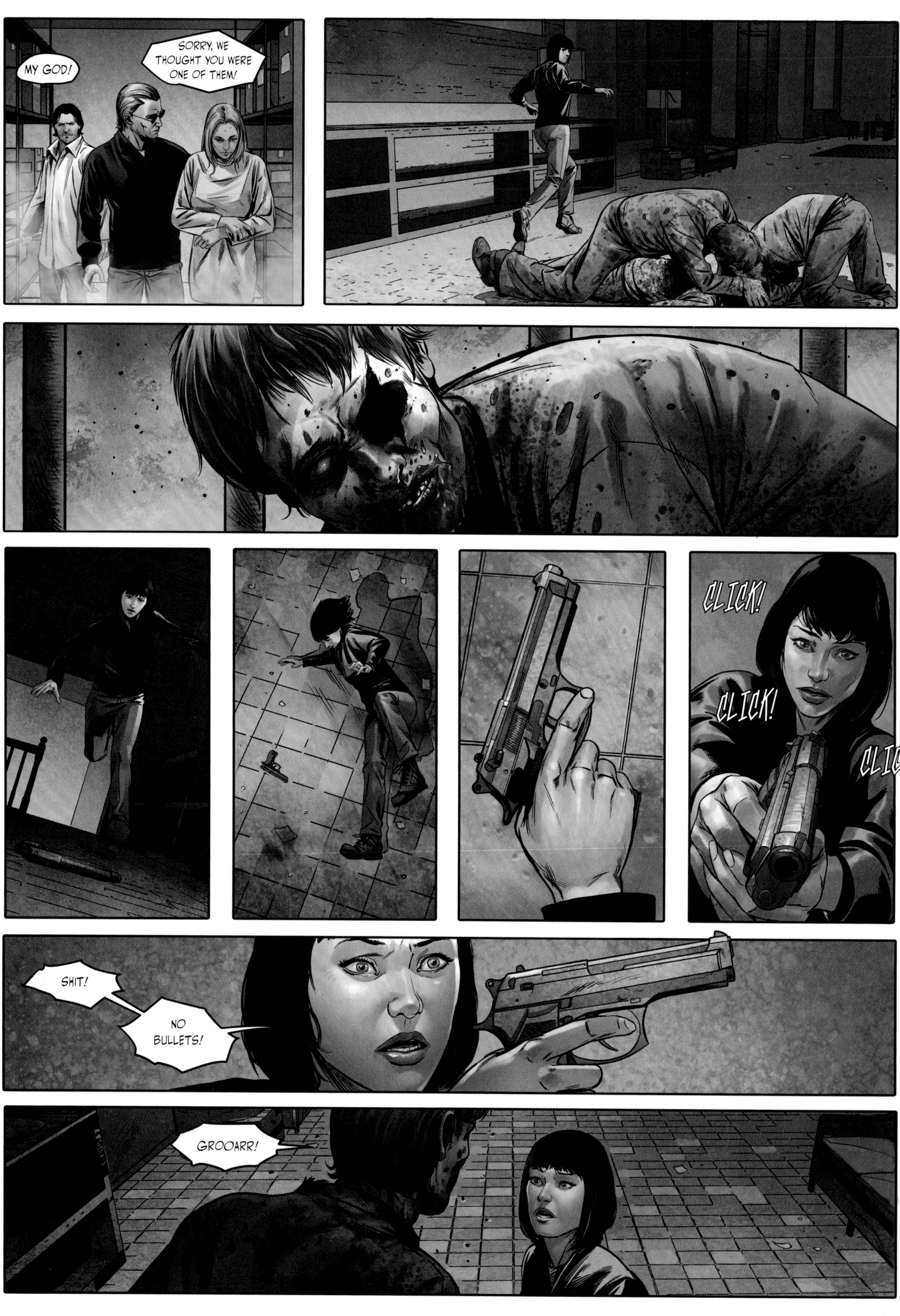
MY GOD!
SORRY, WE THOUGHT YOU WERE ONE OF THEM!
CLICK!
CLICK!
SHIT!
NO BULLETS!
GROOARR!

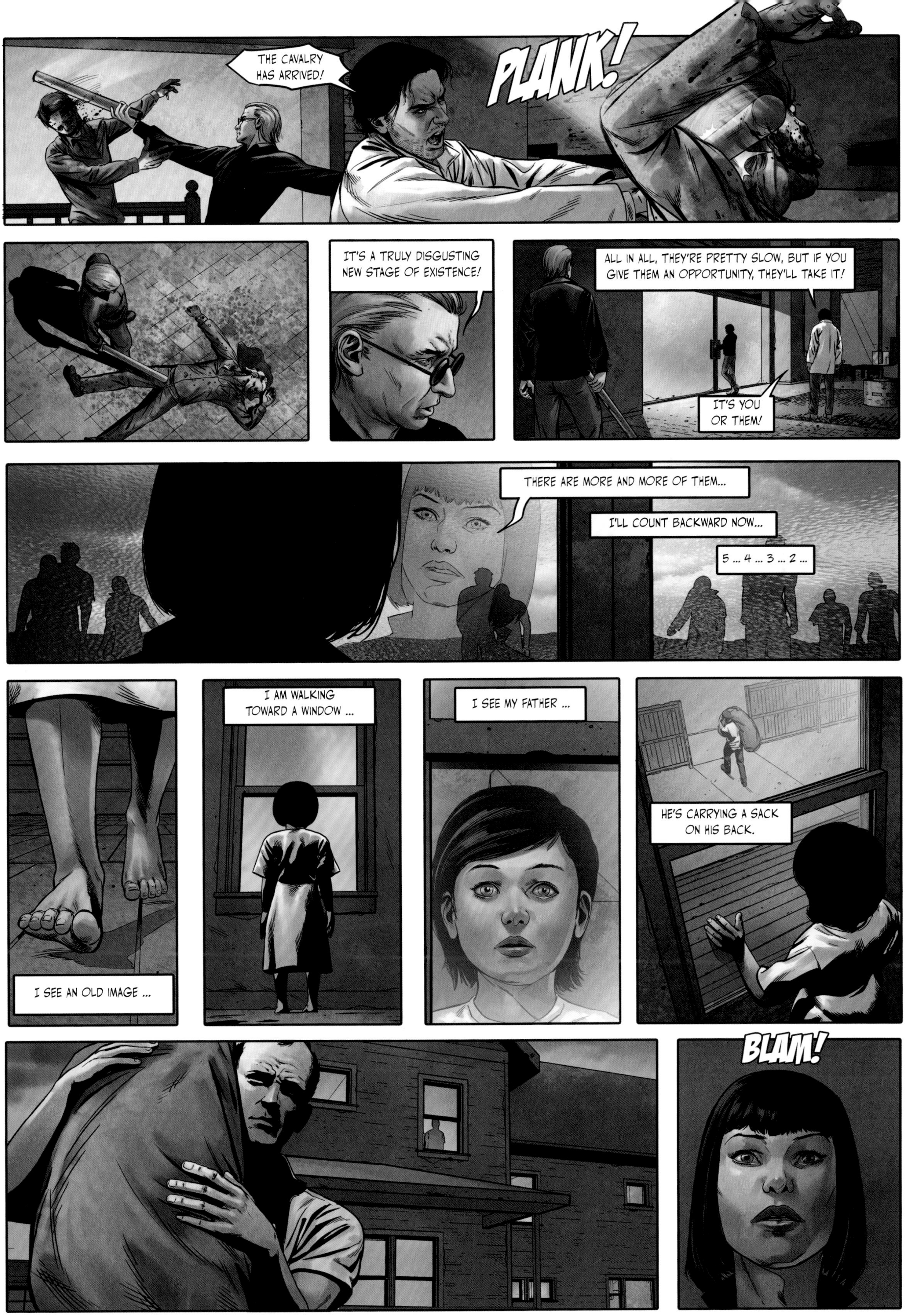
THE CAVALRY HAS ARRIVED!
PLANK!
IT'S A TRULY DISGUSTING NEW STAGE OF EXISTENCE!
ALL IN ALL, THEY'RE PRETTY SLOW, BUT IF YOU GIVE THEM AN OPPORTUNITY, THEY'LL TAKE IT!
IT'S YOU OR THEM!
THERE ARE MORE AND MORE OF THEM...
I'LL COUNT BACKWARD NOW...
5 ... 4 ... 3 ... 2 ...
I SEE AN OLD IMAGE ...
I AM WALKING TOWARD A WINDOW ...
I SEE MY FATHER ...
HE'S CARRYING A SACK ON HIS BACK.
BLAM!

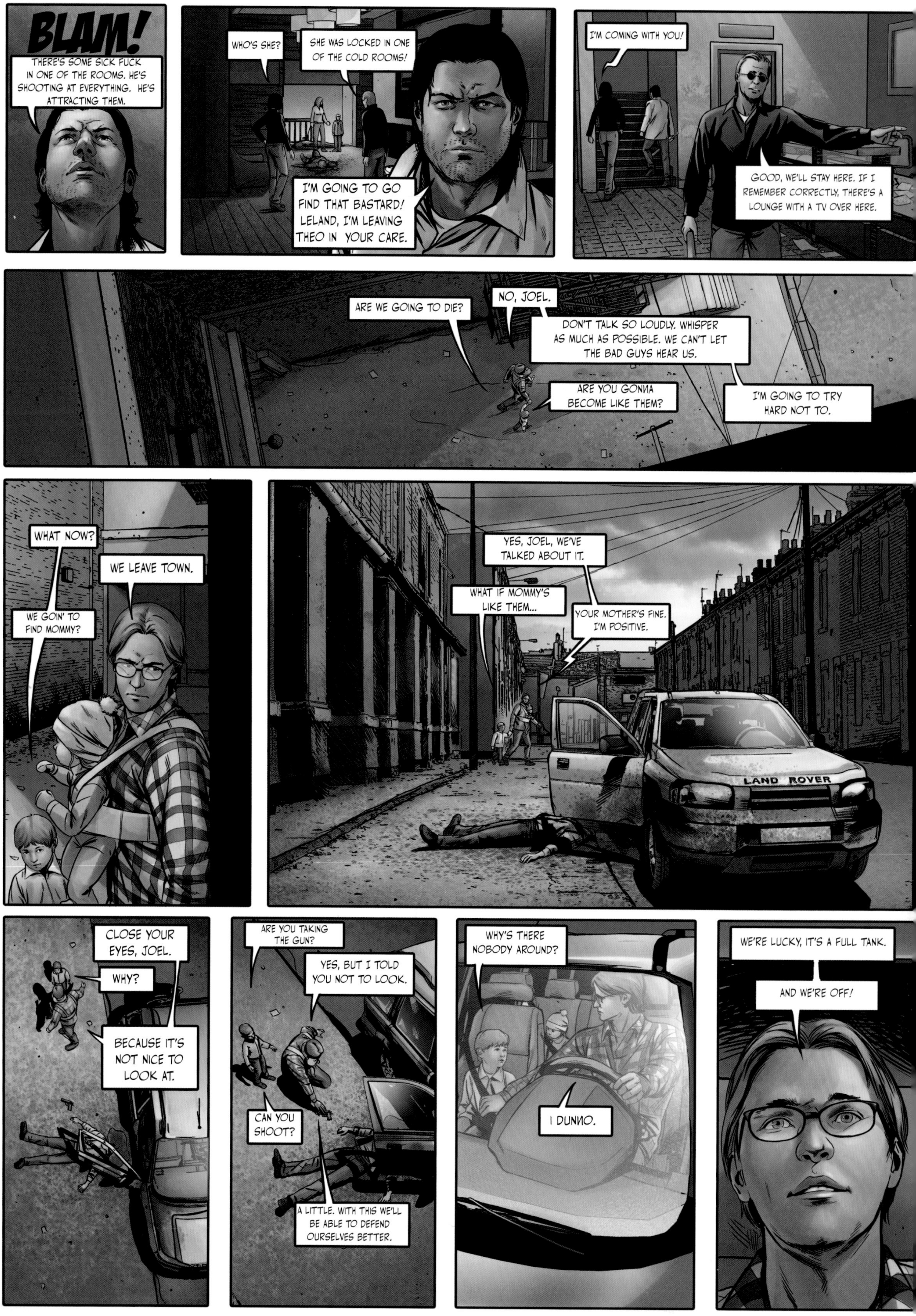
BLAM!
THERE'S SOME SICK FUCK IN ONE OF THE ROOMS. HE'S SHOOTING AT EVERYTHING. HE'S ATTRACTING THEM.
WHO'S SHE?
SHE WAS LOCKED IN ONE OF THE COLD ROOMS!
I'M GOING TO GO FIND THAT BASTARD! LELAND, I'M LEAVING THEO IN YOUR CARE.
I'M COMING WITH YOU!
GOOD, WE'LL STAY HERE. IF I REMEMBER CORRECTLY, THERE'S A LOUNGE WITH A TV OVER HERE.
ARE WE GOING TO DIE?
NO, JOEL.
DON'T TALK SO LOUDLY. WHISPER AS MUCH AS POSSIBLE. WE CAN'T LET THE BAD GUYS HEAR US.
ARE YOU GONNA BECOME LIKE THEM?
I'M GOING TO TRY HARD NOT TO.
WHAT NOW?
WE LEAVE TOWN.
WE GOIN' TO FIND MOMMY?
YES, JOEL, WE'VE TALKED ABOUT IT.
WHAT IF MOMMY'S LIKE THEM...
YOUR MOTHER'S FINE. I'M POSITIVE.
LAND ROVER
CLOSE YOUR EYES, JOEL.
WHY?
BECAUSE IT'S NOT NICE TO LOOK AT.
ARE YOU TAKING THE GUN?
YES, BUT I TOLD YOU NOT TO LOOK.
CAN YOU SHOOT?
A LITTLE. WITH THIS WE'LL BE ABLE TO DEFEND OURSELVES BETTER.
WHY'S THERE NOBODY AROUND?
I DUNNO.
WE'RE LUCKY, IT'S A FULL TANK.
AND WE'RE OFF!

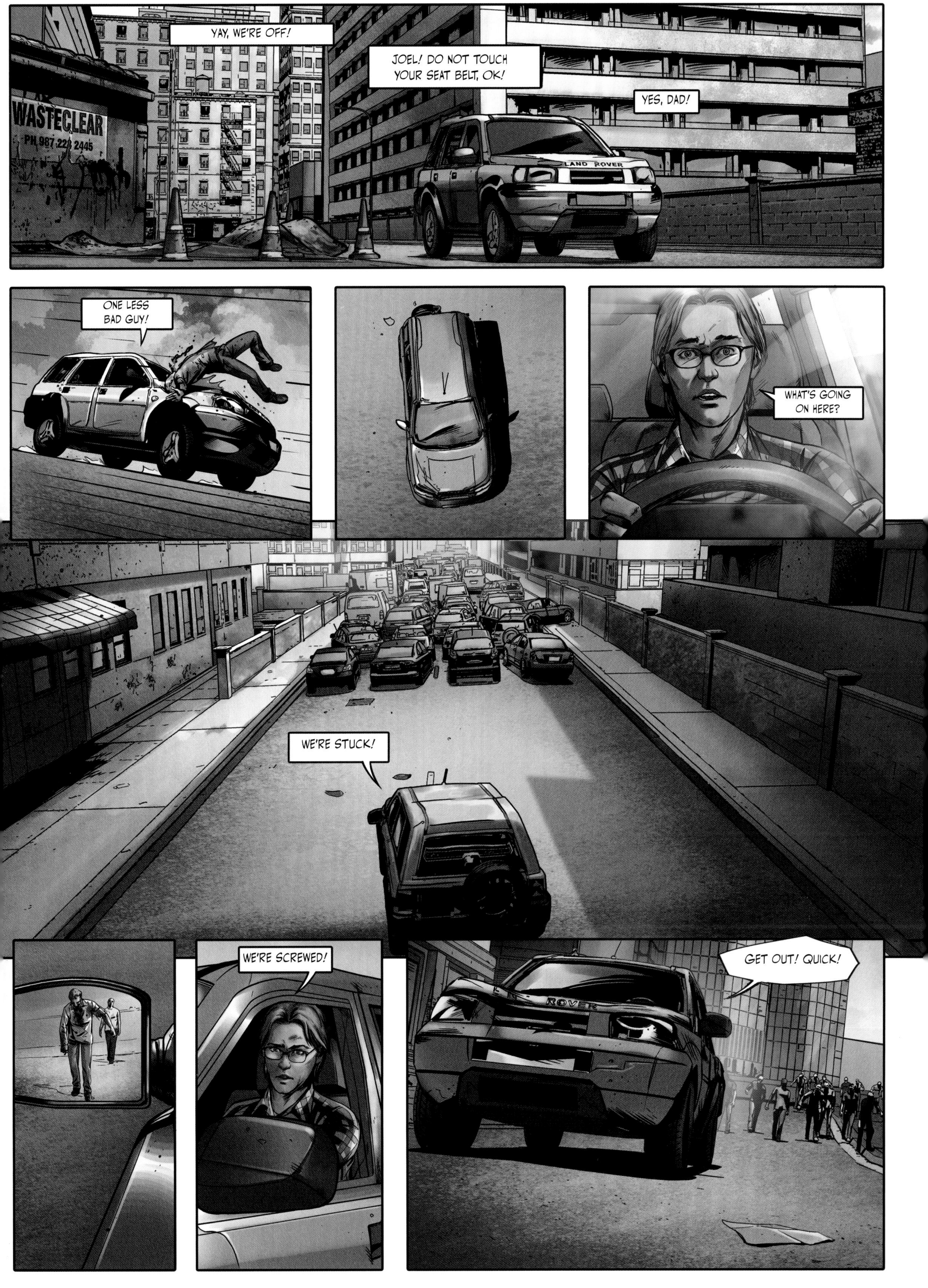
WASTECLEAR
PH 987 223 2445
YAY, WE'RE OFF!
JOEL! DO NOT TOUCH YOUR SEAT BELT, OK!
YES, DAD!
LAND ROVER
ONE LESS BAD GUY!
WHAT'S GOING ON HERE?
WE'RE STUCK!
WE'RE SCREWED!
ROVER
GET OUT! QUICK!

COME ON, SAME AS LAST TIME GET ON MY BACK.

I'M SCARED!

ME TOO. BUT WE'LL HOLD OUR EARS!

WHY?

BECAUSE IT'S GOING TO BE LOUD!

BLAM!

BLAM! BLAM!

HEYYOOOO!

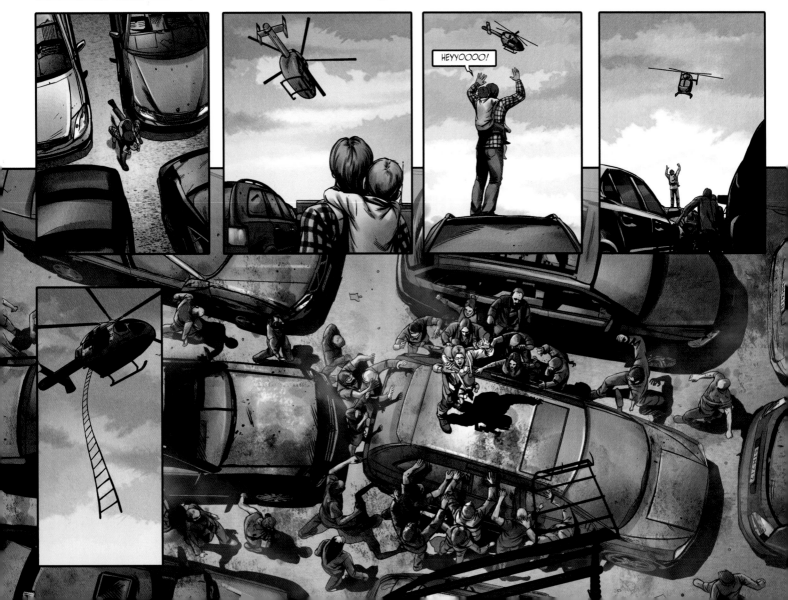

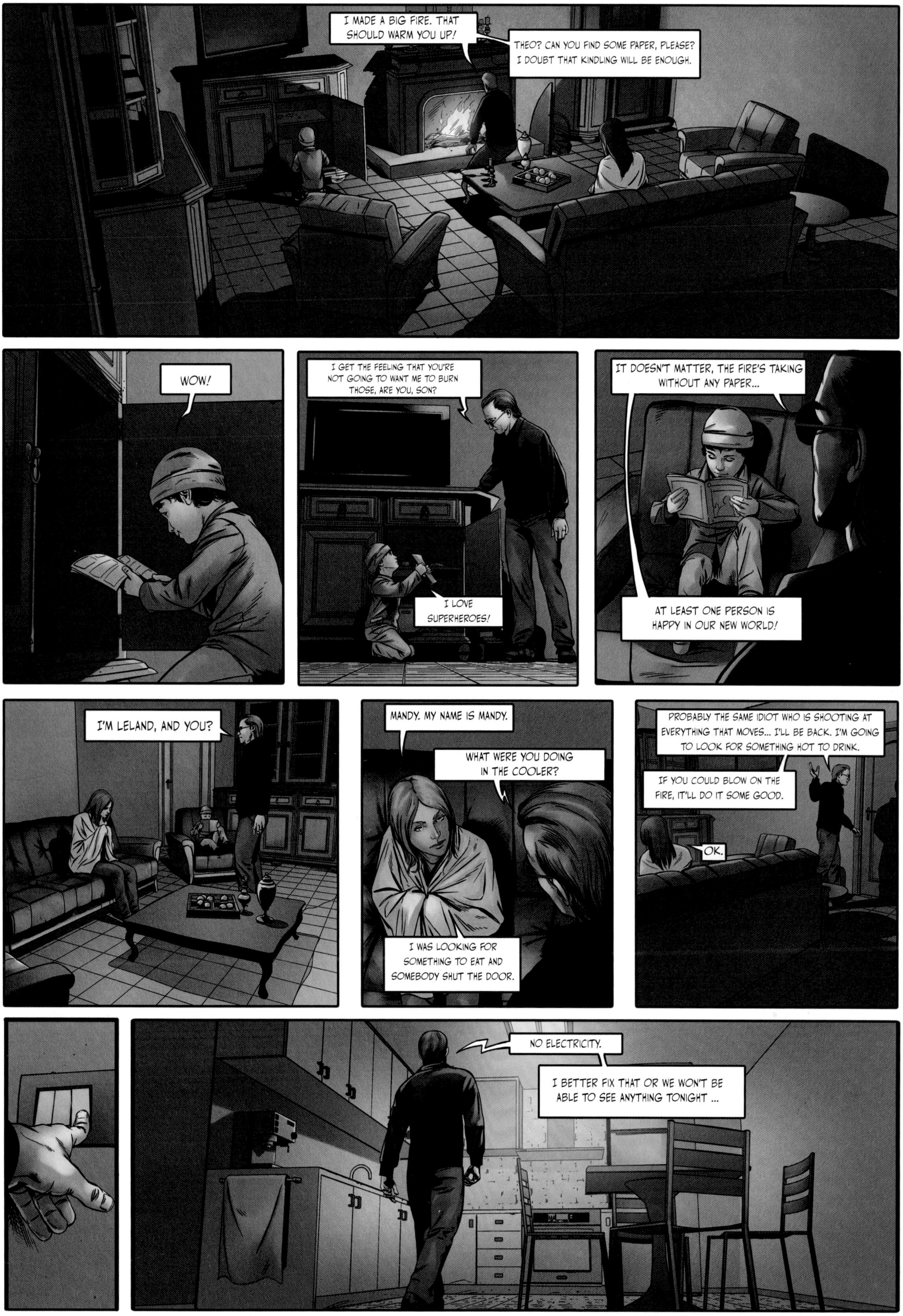
I MADE A BIG FIRE. THAT SHOULD WARM YOU UP!
THEO? CAN YOU FIND SOME PAPER, PLEASE? I DOUBT THAT KINDLING WILL BE ENOUGH.
WOW!
I GET THE FEELING THAT YOU'RE NOT GOING TO WANT ME TO BURN THOSE, ARE YOU, SON?
I LOVE SUPERHEROES!
IT DOESN'T MATTER, THE FIRE'S TAKING WITHOUT ANY PAPER...
AT LEAST ONE PERSON IS HAPPY IN OUR NEW WORLD!
I'M LELAND, AND YOU?
MANDY. MY NAME IS MANDY.
WHAT WERE YOU DOING IN THE COOLER?
I WAS LOOKING FOR SOMETHING TO EAT AND SOMEBODY SHUT THE DOOR.
PROBABLY THE SAME IDIOT WHO IS SHOOTING AT EVERYTHING THAT MOVES... I'LL BE BACK. I'M GOING TO LOOK FOR SOMETHING HOT TO DRINK.
IF YOU COULD BLOW ON THE FIRE, IT'LL DO IT SOME GOOD.
OK.
NO ELECTRICITY.
I BETTER FIX THAT OR WE WON'T BE ABLE TO SEE ANYTHING TONIGHT ...

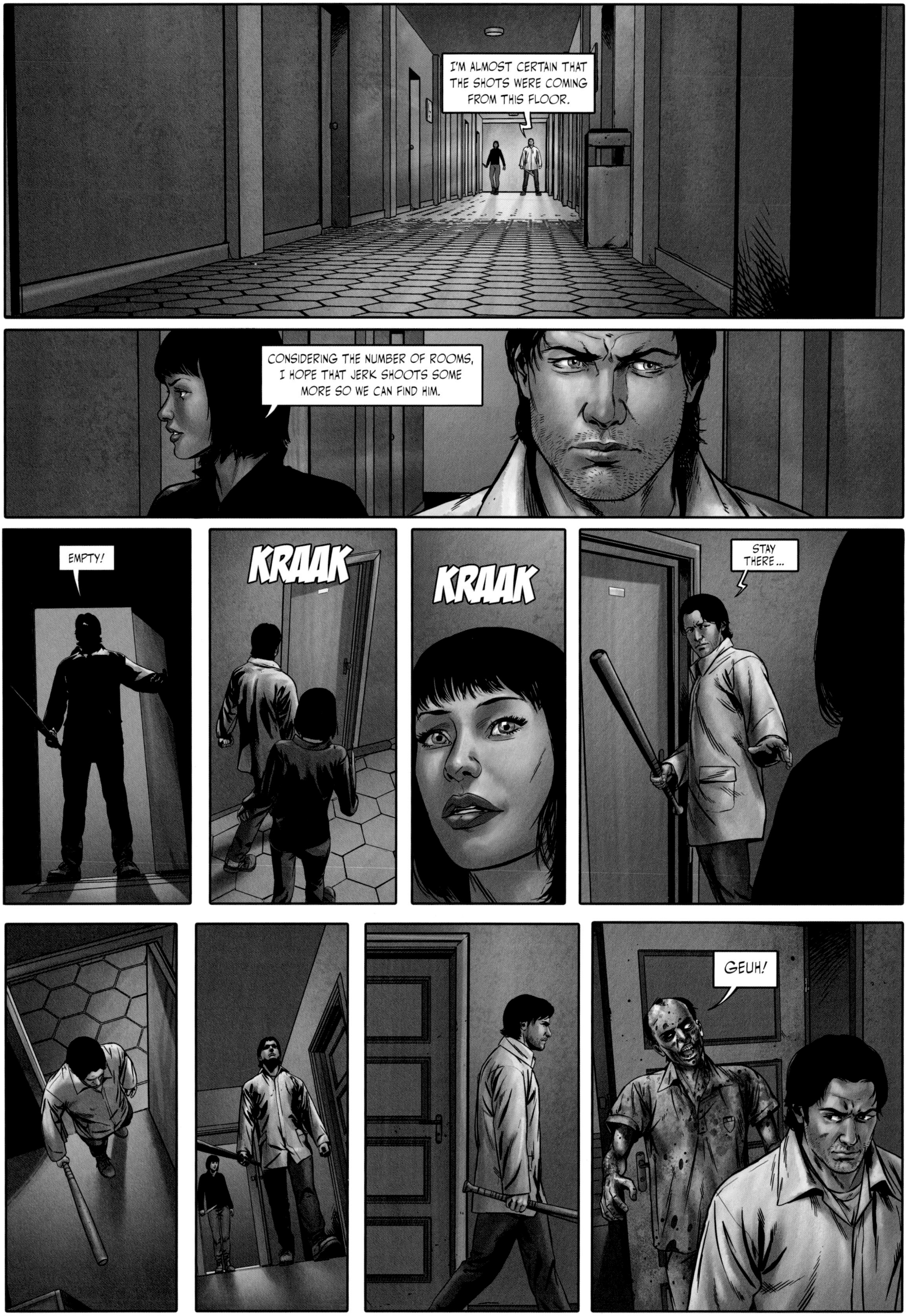
I'M ALMOST CERTAIN THAT THE SHOTS WERE COMING FROM THIS FLOOR.
CONSIDERING THE NUMBER OF ROOMS, I HOPE THAT JERK SHOOTS SOME MORE SO WE CAN FIND HIM.
EMPTY!
KRAAK
KRAAK
STAY THERE...
GEUH!

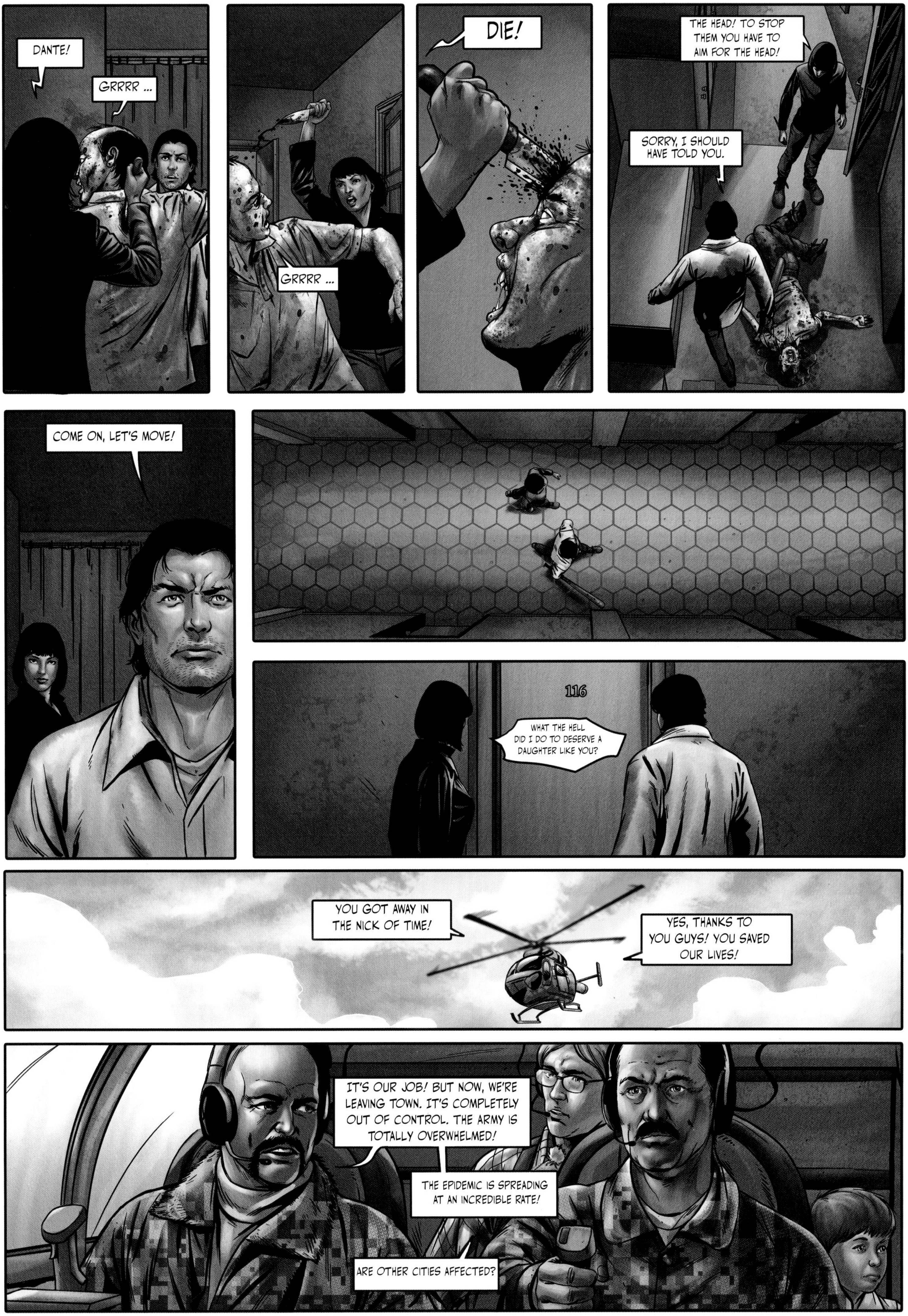
DANTE!
GRRRR ...
GRRRR ...
DIE!
THE HEAD! TO STOP THEM YOU HAVE TO AIM FOR THE HEAD!
SORRY, I SHOULD HAVE TOLD YOU.
COME ON, LET'S MOVE!
116
WHAT THE HELL DID I DO TO DESERVE A DAUGHTER LIKE YOU?
YOU GOT AWAY IN THE NICK OF TIME!
YES, THANKS TO YOU GUYS! YOU SAVED OUR LIVES!
IT'S OUR JOB! BUT NOW, WE'RE LEAVING TOWN. IT'S COMPLETELY OUT OF CONTROL. THE ARMY IS TOTALLY OVERWHELMED!
THE EPIDEMIC IS SPREADING AT AN INCREDIBLE RATE!
ARE OTHER CITIES AFFECTED?

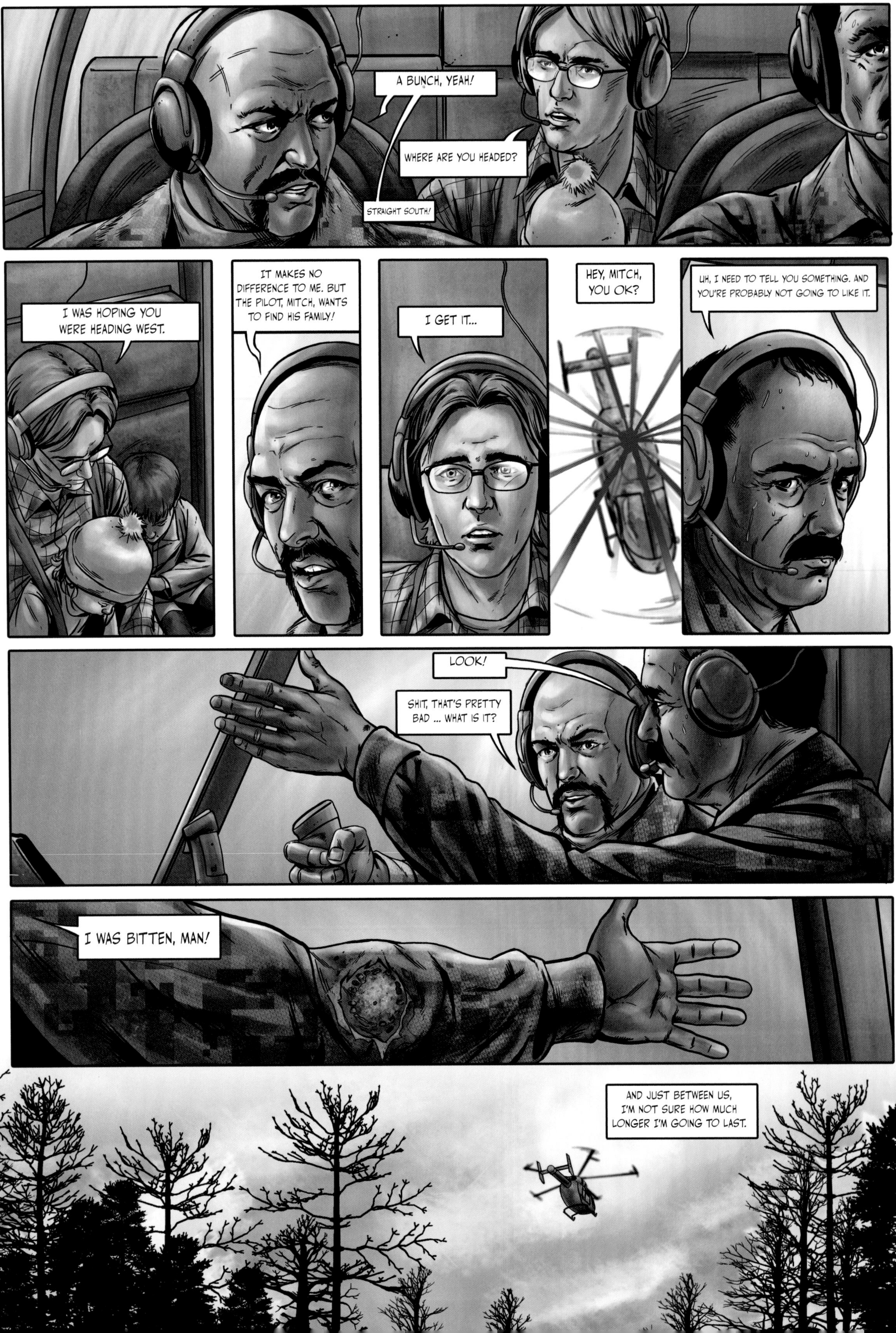
A BUNCH, YEAH!
WHERE ARE YOU HEADED?
STRAIGHT SOUTH!
I WAS HOPING YOU WERE HEADING WEST.
IT MAKES NO DIFFERENCE TO ME. BUT THE PILOT, MITCH, WANTS TO FIND HIS FAMILY!
I GET IT...
HEY, MITCH, YOU OK?
UH, I NEED TO TELL YOU SOMETHING. AND YOU'RE PROBABLY NOT GOING TO LIKE IT.
LOOK!
SHIT, THAT'S PRETTY BAD ... WHAT IS IT?
I WAS BITTEN, MAN!
AND JUST BETWEEN US, I'M NOT SURE HOW MUCH LONGER I'M GOING TO LAST.

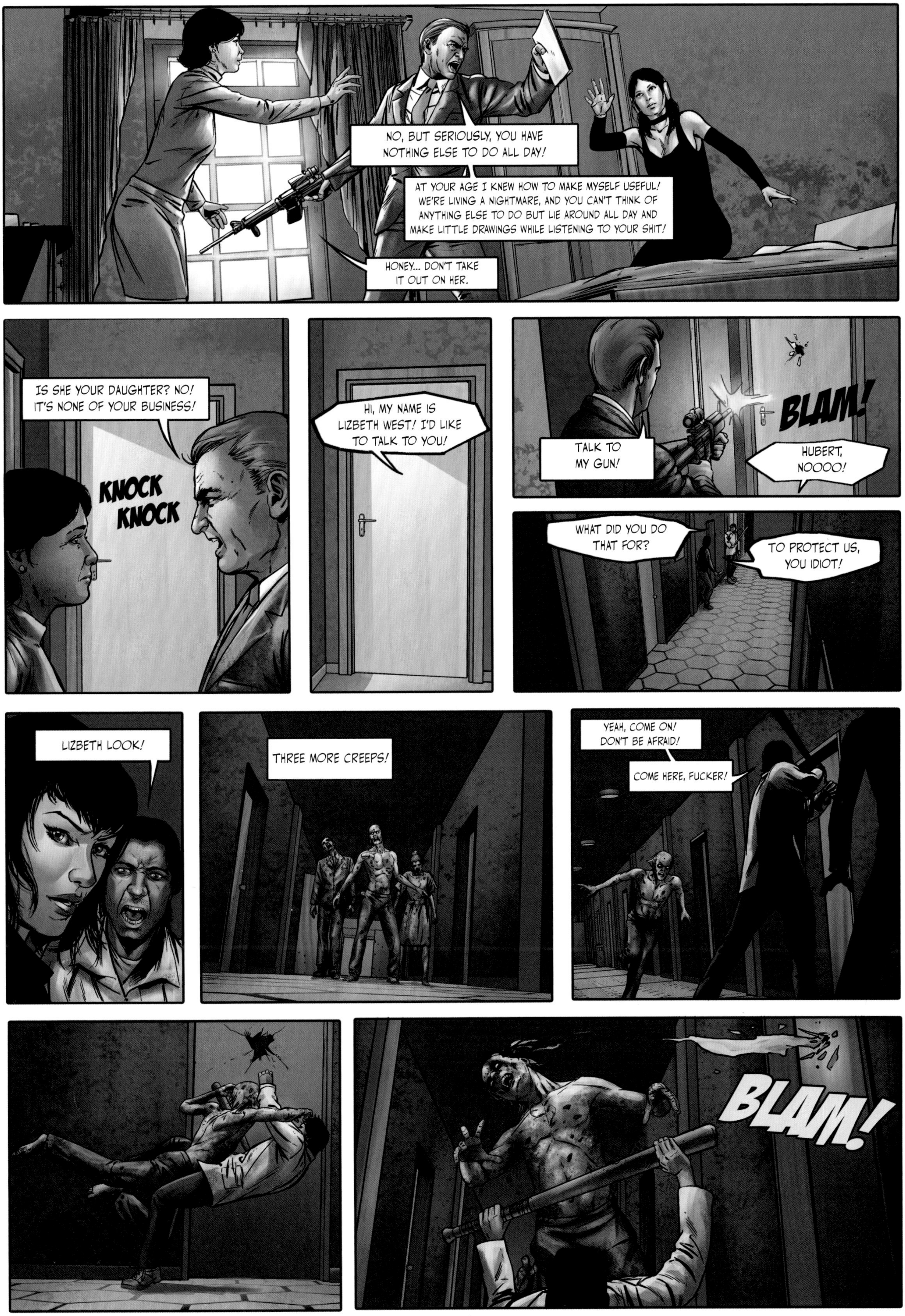
NO, BUT SERIOUSLY, YOU HAVE NOTHING ELSE TO DO ALL DAY!
AT YOUR AGE I KNEW HOW TO MAKE MYSELF USEFUL! WE'RE LIVING A NIGHTMARE, AND YOU CAN'T THINK OF ANYTHING ELSE TO DO BUT LIE AROUND ALL DAY AND MAKE LITTLE DRAWINGS WHILE LISTENING TO YOUR SHIT!
HONEY... DON'T TAKE IT OUT ON HER.
IS SHE YOUR DAUGHTER? NO! IT'S NONE OF YOUR BUSINESS!
KNOCK KNOCK
HI, MY NAME IS LIZBETH WEST! I'D LIKE TO TALK TO YOU!
TALK TO MY GUN!
BLAM!
HUBERT, NOOOO!
WHAT DID YOU DO THAT FOR?
TO PROTECT US, YOU IDIOT!
LIZBETH LOOK!
THREE MORE CREEPS!
YEAH, COME ON! DON'T BE AFRAID!
COME HERE, FUCKER!
BLAM!

I'M BEGGING YOU! OPEN THE DOOR!
WE'RE GOING TO HAVE TO DO OUR OWN HOUSEKEEPING!
I NEED TO FIND A CLEANER WEAPON. I'M GETTING THEM ALL OVER MY HANDS EVERY TIME!
A CLEAN WEAPON! IS THERE SUCH A THING?
I'M GOING TO STRANGLE THAT GUY!
DAD...
YES, HONEY?
ARE WE THERE YET?
IN A FEW MINUTES, LITTLE MAN.
I WANT A KISS!
SMACK
MITCH?

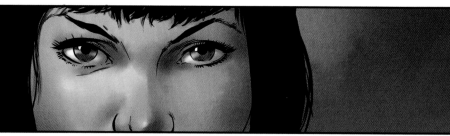

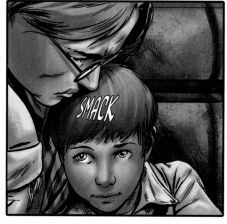

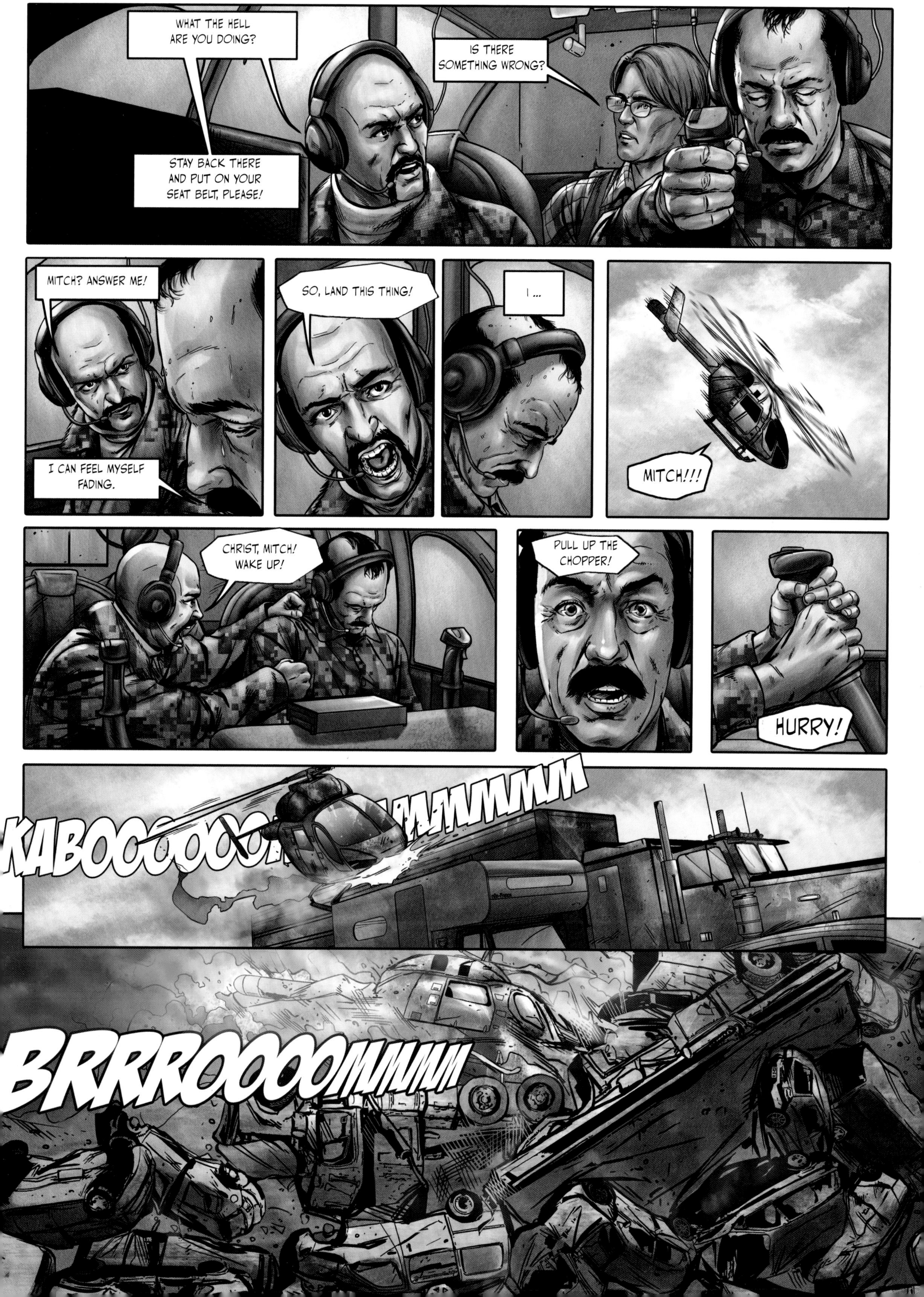
WHAT THE HELL ARE YOU DOING?
STAY BACK THERE AND PUT ON YOUR SEAT BELT, PLEASE!
IS THERE SOMETHING WRONG?
MITCH? ANSWER ME!
I CAN FEEL MYSELF FADING.
SO, LAND THIS THING!
I ...
MITCH!!!
CHRIST, MITCH! WAKE UP!
PULL UP THE CHOPPER!
HURRY!
KABOOOOOOOMMMMMMM
BRRROOOOMMMM

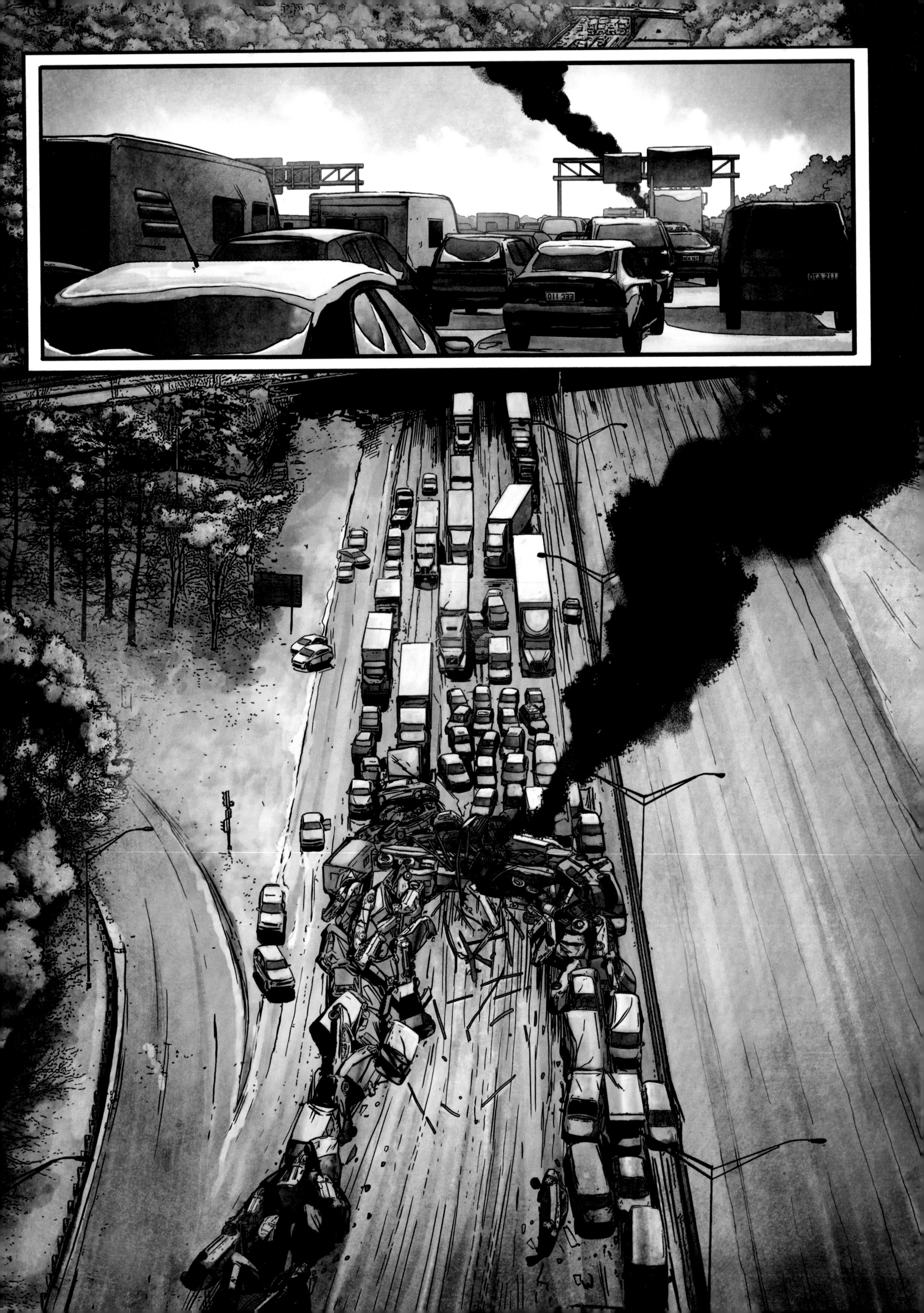

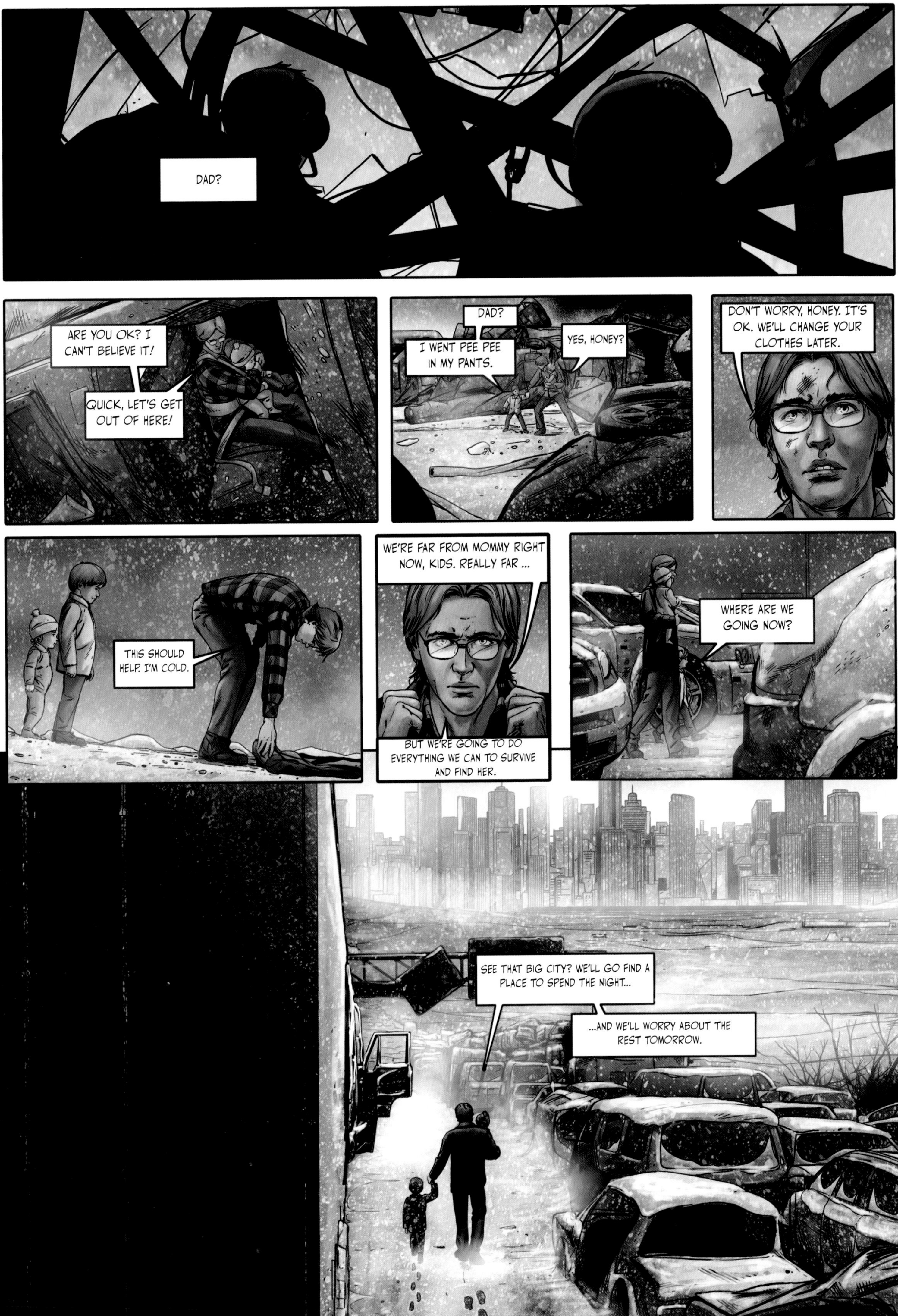
DAD?
ARE YOU OK? I CAN'T BELIEVE IT!
QUICK, LET'S GET OUT OF HERE!
DAD?
YES, HONEY?
I WENT PEE PEE IN MY PANTS.
DON'T WORRY, HONEY. IT'S OK. WE'LL CHANGE YOUR CLOTHES LATER.
THIS SHOULD HELP. I'M COLD.
WE'RE FAR FROM MOMMY RIGHT NOW, KIDS. REALLY FAR ...
BUT WE'RE GOING TO DO EVERYTHING WE CAN TO SURVIVE AND FIND HER.
WHERE ARE WE GOING NOW?
SEE THAT BIG CITY? WE'LL GO FIND A PLACE TO SPEND THE NIGHT...
...AND WE'LL WORRY ABOUT THE REST TOMORROW.

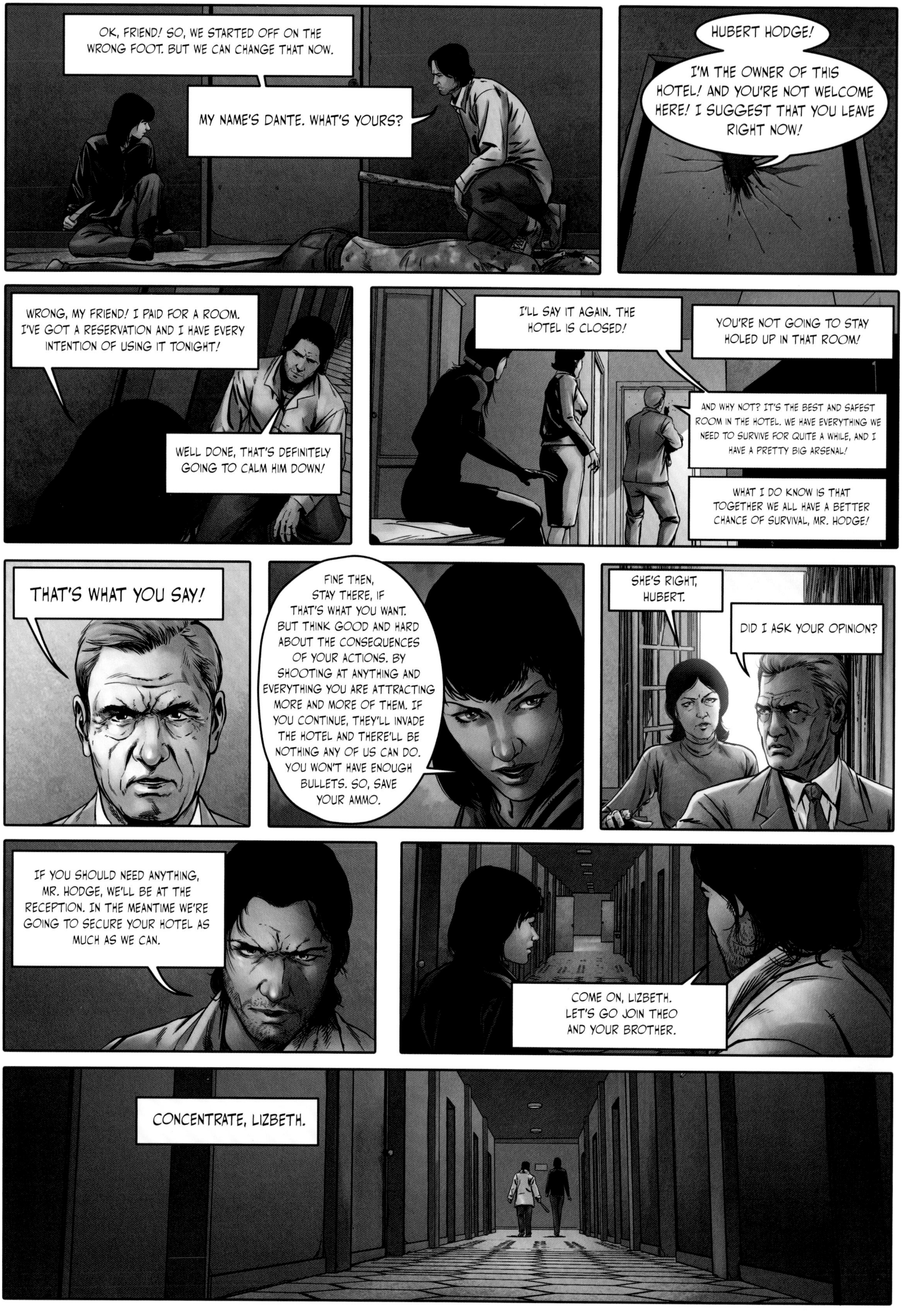
OK, FRIEND! SO, WE STARTED OFF ON THE WRONG FOOT. BUT WE CAN CHANGE THAT NOW.
MY NAME'S DANTE. WHAT'S YOURS?
HUBERT HODGE!
I'M THE OWNER OF THIS HOTEL! AND YOU'RE NOT WELCOME HERE! I SUGGEST THAT YOU LEAVE RIGHT NOW!
WRONG, MY FRIEND! I PAID FOR A ROOM. I'VE GOT A RESERVATION AND I HAVE EVERY INTENTION OF USING IT TONIGHT!
WELL DONE, THAT'S DEFINITELY GOING TO CALM HIM DOWN!
I'LL SAY IT AGAIN. THE HOTEL IS CLOSED!
YOU'RE NOT GOING TO STAY HOLED UP IN THAT ROOM!
AND WHY NOT? IT'S THE BEST AND SAFEST ROOM IN THE HOTEL. WE HAVE EVERYTHING WE NEED TO SURVIVE FOR QUITE A WHILE, AND I HAVE A PRETTY BIG ARSENAL!
WHAT I DO KNOW IS THAT TOGETHER WE ALL HAVE A BETTER CHANCE OF SURVIVAL, MR. HODGE!
THAT'S WHAT YOU SAY!
FINE THEN, STAY THERE, IF THAT'S WHAT YOU WANT. BUT THINK GOOD AND HARD ABOUT THE CONSEQUENCES OF YOUR ACTIONS. BY SHOOTING AT ANYTHING AND EVERYTHING YOU ARE ATTRACTING MORE AND MORE OF THEM. IF YOU CONTINUE, THEY'LL INVADE THE HOTEL AND THERE'LL BE NOTHING ANY OF US CAN DO. YOU WON'T HAVE ENOUGH BULLETS. SO, SAVE YOUR AMMO.
SHE'S RIGHT, HUBERT.
DID I ASK YOUR OPINION?
IF YOU SHOULD NEED ANYTHING, MR. HODGE, WE'LL BE AT THE RECEPTION. IN THE MEANTIME WE'RE GOING TO SECURE YOUR HOTEL AS MUCH AS WE CAN.
COME ON, LIZBETH. LET'S GO JOIN THEO AND YOUR BROTHER.
CONCENTRATE, LIZBETH.

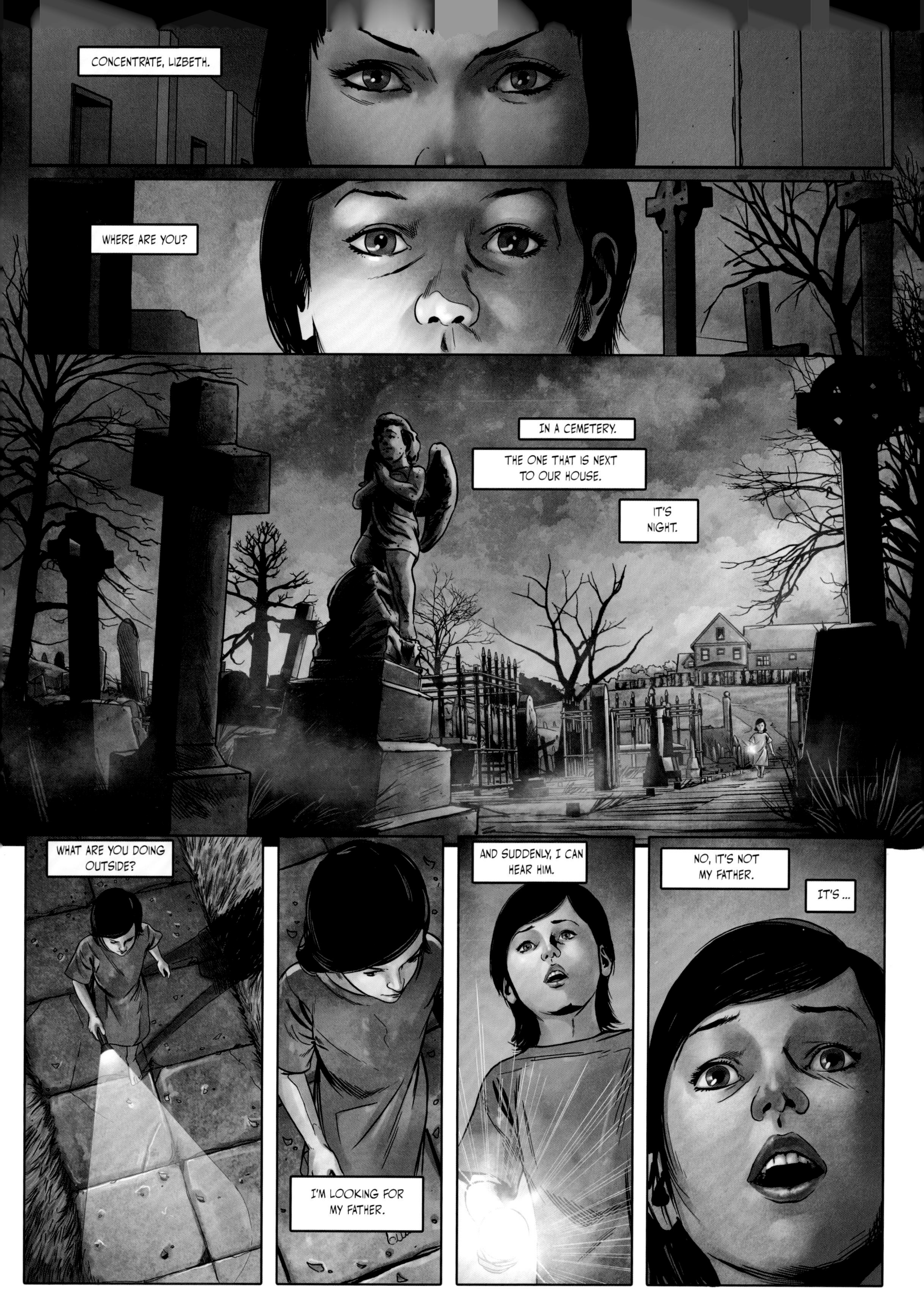
CONCENTRATE, LIZBETH.
WHERE ARE YOU?
IN A CEMETERY.
THE ONE THAT IS NEXT TO OUR HOUSE.
IT'S NIGHT.
WHAT ARE YOU DOING OUTSIDE?
I'M LOOKING FOR MY FATHER.
AND SUDDENLY, I CAN HEAR HIM.
NO, IT'S NOT MY FATHER.
IT'S ...

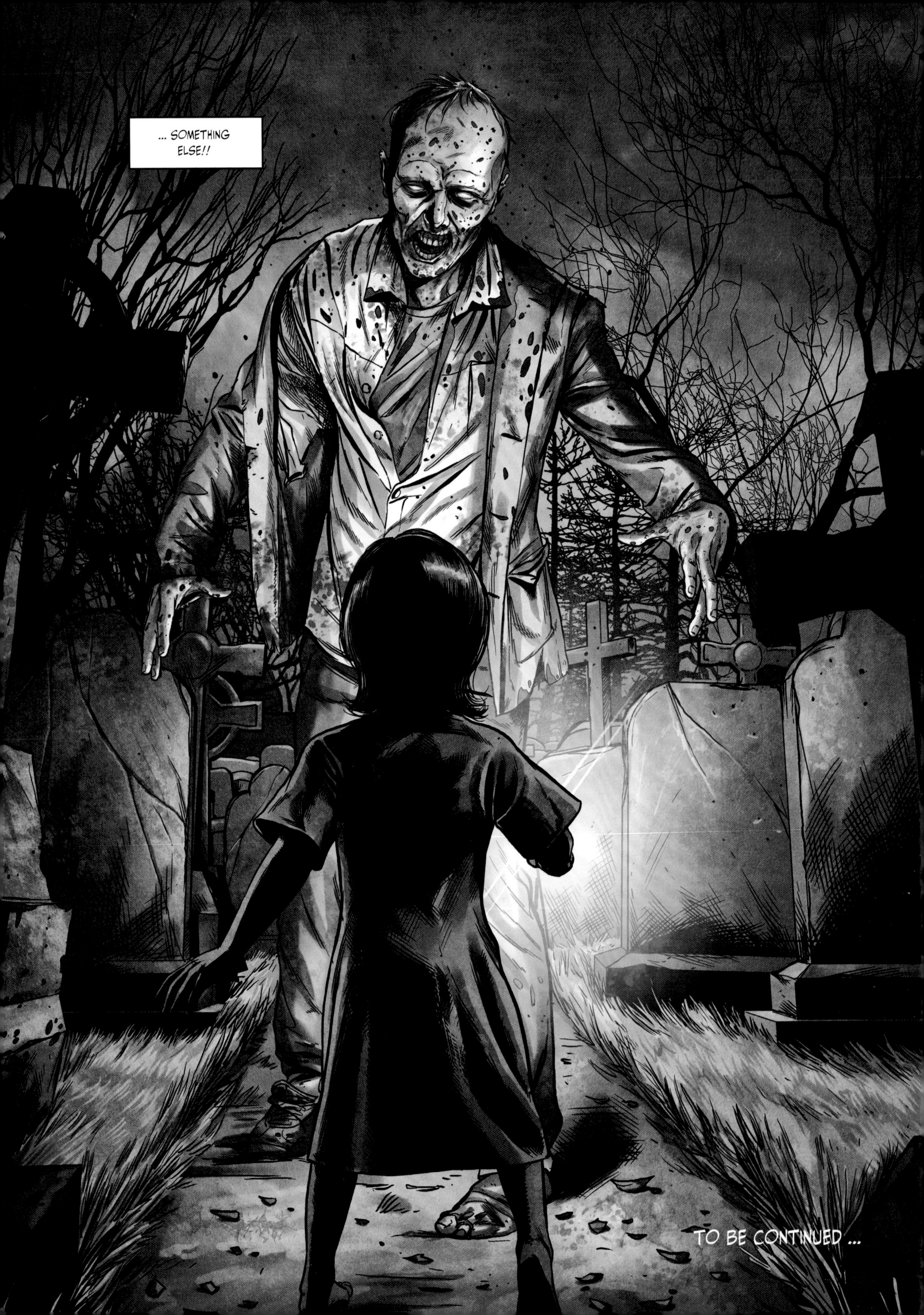
... SOMETHING ELSE!!
TO BE CONTINUED ...